*T*ESTIMONY from the Belloc's *Economics for* ~~Helen~~

"This highly original and perceptive book should be read by everyone who has any interest in the just functioning of markets. Hilaire Belloc's analysis of the processes of production, exchange, and consumption displays a profundity that is belied by the brevity of the book, and a faithfulness to a Catholic worldview that is sadly all too rare in books on this topic."

—Andrew Abela, Ph.D.
Professor of Marketing, Catholic University of America

"In another era of economic uncertainty, Hilaire Belloc's *Economics for Helen* provided readers with an insightful introduction to both economic theory and policy. Rejecting the prevailing economic trends of mammoth industrial capitalism and state socialism, Belloc's economics offered a prudent alternative on a human scale that was rooted in the relationship between small property, freedom, and human happiness. Thanks to IHS Press for making this leg of Belloc's economic trilogy – *The Servile State, Economics for Helen,* and *The Restoration of Property* – available again to readers more than three-quarters of a century after it first appeared."

—Andrew W. Foshee, Ph.D.
Professor of Economics, McNeese State University

"Even after 75 + years this book is a worthwhile read. The first part presents a clear and jargon-free exposition of the economic theory that was mainstream then and now. In the remainder of the book he uses it not to defend the capitalist economy, as economists do, but to demonstrate how it falls short of a just system. It does so because capital is owned by so few. As an alternative, he outlines the 'Distributive State' where the ownership of labor, capital, and land is widely distributed. Belloc still has much to teach us about the nature of a good society."

—Charles K. Wilber, Ph.D.
Emeritus Professor of Economics, University of Notre Dame

"In *Economics for Helen* Hillare Belloc presents an informed and entertaining introduction into the important subject of the economy, an accomplishment that few modern textbooks on the subject can claim. What I mean by informed is that Belloc's approach to economics is informed by an accurate understanding of the nature of the human person and the family (in contrast to the 'rational economic man' nonsense so common in economic textbooks), the necessary building blocks for society and social analysis. What is most unique about Belloc's approach to economics is that he never forgets that economics is about people and not numbers, and that economic actions and outcomes are moral actions and outcomes. This is particularly evident in his treatment of wealth, which is closer to the mark than anything neoclassical economics has to offer."

—Charles M. A. Clark, Ph.D.
    Senior Fellow, Vincentian Center for Church and Society and
    Professor of Economics, St. John's University

"...a well-written, almost folksy journey through the Economics discipline.

"...One of the book's more appealing points is that Belloc seldom takes strong positions on particular topics, but is rather content to mention what others have to say. However, when he does take issue with a certain view, he argues his case carefully and persuasively. Such balance is welcome in a field where political opinion often masquerades as fact."

—David Rajnes
    A federal-government economist working in Washington, DC

"This is a challenging primer for young economists. Belloc outlines the core issues that the common man expects from economics and provides his (sometimes idiosyncratic) solutions. It should be read by persons who want to reflect on the fundamental social questions of economics and by economists who are willing to meet the challenge of what is expected of them."

—Dr. Garrick Small
    Head of Property Studies Department, University of
    Technology Studies, Sydney, Australia

"This book offers a rare glimpse of Belloc's thought on the whole of economic theory in the 1920s. Pedagogically, Belloc is a master of complementing the abstract principles of economics with everyday examples that make the subject matter accessible and relevant. Many modern treatments of the subject could learn from that approach. The book is of interest because it reveals Belloc's view of the capitalist system in the era of the big trusts. The need for reform of the capitalistic system was at that time obvious, but reading an analysis from an informed contemporary was an eye-opening experience. The chapter on the Distributive State is most thought-provoking, because Belloc systematically describes both the benefits of and obstacles to the system, including even such modern concerns as the capability to innovate and the problems of generating revenue. The concept of productive and unproductive loans employed to define usury properly has modern applications for distinguishing between business and consumer loans. Overall, reading Belloc is a pleasure because regardless of the subject matter one learns greatly about the history and culture of the British people. I highly recommend this book for those who are interested in the economic thought of Hilaire Belloc."

> —Guillermo Montes, Ph.D.
> Associate Professor of Economics, Ave Maria University

"Belloc understood the essentials of economics and presents them in his clear, entertaining, and inimitable style. His pithy primer explains the underlying truths of economics as few 'professional' economists have and places them in the indispensable moral context that gives them human meaning. The 'back to basics' beginner text for young and old is neither dated, dry, nor 'dismal.'"

> —Timothy J. Cullen
> former equities trader and partner, Cold Mountain Capital Management

"In college courses that feature the 'economics of reality,' such as mine on Economic Geography, *Economics for Helen* is unparalleled in the resonance of its explanation. I will use this book to enlighten my students for years to come."

> —James Knotwell, Ph.D.
> Assistant Professor, Dept. of History, Politics, and Geography, Wayne State College

"*Economics for Helen* offers some interesting and novel ways to illustrate basic economic concepts. ...it would be helpful to someone who wants to know more about economic organization, and who wants a less technical presentation than a modern economist normally would provide. I also found the presentation of Distributism helpful in understanding what is meant by the term – a term most modern economists do not know in the way Belloc and Chesterton used the term."

> —John Lunn, Ph.D.
> Robert W. Haack Professor of Economics, Hope College

"This new edition of Belloc's text on economics is most welcome, for it contains much common sense and a clarity in logic and fact that would resolve much of the economic illiteracy so prevalent these days. The man on the street without an ounce of economic education would benefit equally along with the policy analyst, the pundit, and, dare I say, the professional economist. I plan to adopt the text as required auxiliary reading in a range of economics courses I regularly teach."

—Michael Welker, Ph.D.
Assistant Professor of Economics, Franciscan University of Steubenville

"Although the economic doctrines of the Austrian School may appear superior to socialism, it is folly to insist either has the true happiness of society in view. What does is Catholic Social Teaching. One of its most observant and capable apologists is Hilaire Belloc."

—Robert Boehm, M.B.A.
Chartered Life Underwriter, Chartered Financial Consultant, and former Libertarian who spent 12 years studying Austrian economics at the Foundation for Economic Education

"*Economics for Helen* represents what is lacking in most modern-day treatments of basic economics: a comprehensive treatment of the subject, including cogent coverage of Distributism (missing from, or impugned by, many contemporary texts). A must for anyone who really wants to *learn* economics. A Belloc jewel in the rough!"

—Kevin M. Bryant, Ph.D.
Associate Professor of Sociology, Benedictine College

"...the smaller government that many on the Right desire is better achieved through Distributism.... At the same time, [it] produces a more even distribution of wealth in society...the Left would [also] be far more pleased.

"In light of these virtues, it is time that Distributism be given another look. And there's no better place to start than with *Economics for Helen.*"

—Anthony Santelli II, Ph.D.
President, AES Capital Management, L.L.C.

"You will discover no finer primer for those who, like myself, find books on economics soporiferous. *Economics for Helen* reads today as it did twenty years ago when first I read it: fresh and chock-full of deadly insights."

—Scott J. Bloch
Secretary, Hilaire Belloc Society, Washington, D.C.

ECONOMICS FOR HELEN

To our crusading Australian friends at what was (and essentially remains) Bob Santamaria's National Civic Council. With sincere good wishes, heartfelt gratitude, prayerful support, and generous hope for the future. Keep the Faith!

ECONOMICS

for Helen

BY HILAIRE BELLOC

A BRIEF OUTLINE OF REAL ECONOMY

Foreword by Dr. Alberto Piedra
Introduction by Dr. Edward A. McPhail

Norfolk, VA
2004

Economics for Helen was first published by J.W. Arrowsmith of London
in March, 1924, in a limited edition of 265 numbered copies, of which
250 were for sale. The second, popular edition was released at the same
time.

Notes to the original text have been included as footnotes. Original
illustrations have been accurately reproduced, except for the accompanying
text which has been re-typeset. The original formatting, spelling, and
punctuation have been largely preserved in the present edition, aside from
minor editorial corrections.

ISBN: 0-9718286-7-9

Library of Congress Cataloging-in-Publication Data

Belloc, Hilaire, 1870-1953.
   Economics for Helen / by Hilaire Belloc.
      p. cm.
   ISBN 0-932528-03-2
   1. Economics. 2. Wealth. I. Title.
   HB171.B354 2004
   330--dc22

                                                        2003023417
Printed in the United States of America.

IHS Press is the only publisher dedicated exclusively
to the Social Teachings of the Catholic Church.
For information on current or future titles, contact IHS Press at:

toll-free phone/fax: 877.447.7737 (877-IHS-PRES)
e-mail: info@ihspress.com

Table of Contents

Table of Contents (cont'd.)

FOREWORD

HILAIRE BELLOC was born in France in 1870 and moved to England at an early age along with his English-born mother. The result was that, although he was immensely proud of his mixed French and English heritage, he was almost wholly educated in England. He attended school at the Birmingham Oratory, and then went to Balliol College at the University of Oxford where he graduated with the highest honors in History.

Because of his sharp mind and intellectual abilities, Belloc could have quite easily chosen a political career, but his vocation led him to the world of writing and literature. As Robert Nisbet wrote in his Introduction to Belloc's *The Servile State:* "There are not many in the long history of English literature who can match either the extent of his published work or the astonishing diversity of subject and style." As a consequence few people have doubted Hilaire Belloc's contribution to the world of literature.

In the field of his historical writings, however, Belloc has been harshly criticized, though more often than not unjustly so – by those who knew perhaps the letter of the subject but wholly missed the spirit, within which lay the vital meaning. In all of his historical writings, Belloc did not hesitate to expound clearly and defend vigorously all the tenets of the Catholic Faith. Thus his Catholicism is reflected with valor and commendable conciseness in such books as *The Great Heresies, How the Reformation Happened,* and *The Crisis of Civilization.* For Belloc, Catholicism was not a purely cerebral or sentimental attachment, but something incarnated in flesh and blood and running through the whole fabric of history.

Belloc's profound consciousness of seminal realities gave all of his writings an urgency and a precision. He shared with his equally remarkable and close friend, G.K. Chesterton, that anguish which characterizes the few privileged souls that are aware of the dangerous trends that threaten the very foundations of our Western civilization.

In the field of economics, Belloc had already forecast the dangers to the Catholic conception of genuine economic independence posed by the ever-increasing role of government, of burgeoning bureaucracy, and of the brutal logic of unrestricted "market forces." This concern was clearly elaborated in his widely acclaimed *The Servile State;* it was further developed in his later works such as *Economics for Helen* and *An Essay on the Restoration of Property.* The latter sought to outline possible ways of combating such trends, primarily by those who held power or who aspired to wield the necessary power to change the course of history, while the former – presented again to the public with this present edition – was a more theoretical work addressed to those who found economics as a subject confusing, but who nevertheless felt that an understanding of it was necessary.

Economics for Helen is not, nor was it intended to be, a scholarly work or a fully rounded treatise on economics, tedious to read and overweighed by extensive footnotes and references. Rather it is a simple, short, well-written book, intended for the layman, clearly and accurately dealing with the major issues of economics, and dealing with its subject not only through abstract explanation but also by the illustrative use of concrete, historical examples.

Belloc's book covers numerous topics that are both essential to an understanding of basic economics and practically significant, even to the present day. In the second part of the book, "Political Applications," Belloc makes his position known on subjects of relevance to his day and ours. Thus we find Belloc as a defender of free trade when it in fact contributes to the increase of wealth and the genuine health of a local area, but its opponent and critic when free trade actually impoverishes that area. With respect to inflation and the debasement of the currency, he emphasizes its perils and how it has been used in a way that equates to the outright confiscation of people's savings. As for banking and the bankers, he accuses them not only of becoming unnaturally powerful, but also of trying to control the public policy of the State. Taxation in general, and the personal income tax especially, also falls under Belloc's criticism. For him the income tax of his time was unjust because "the honest citizen with an established and known position can be bled to the full, while the rogue and the adventurer, the speculator and dealer escape" (p. 145).

One important element of *Economics for Helen* is an explanation of what Belloc sees as the three different ways in which human society can be constituted economically, depending upon how control is exercised over the three factors of production, namely, land, labor and capital. He defines the three ways thus:

1. The Servile State, "the state in which the material Means of Production are the property of men who also own the human agents of Production."

2. The Capitalist State in which "the material Means of Production are the property of a few and the numerous human agents of Production are free, but without Property."

3. The Distributist State, "the state in which the material Means of Production are owned by the free human agents of Production."

Not surprisingly, Belloc was strongly opposed to the Servile State since it "offends our human love of honor and independence, degrading the mass of men."

Belloc was also a vigorous critic of capitalism. He stresses not only its grave disadvantage of insecurity, above all for the masses, but also the great disparity of wealth that it creates: "a greater disparity of wealth than ever the world knew before! It is clear that society in such a condition must be as unstable as an explosive." Though an untrained eye might conclude that how capitalism has evolved historically does not support Belloc's position, a closer look reveals it to be consistent with that of another profound economic mind, the late Professor Joseph Schumpeter of Harvard University. In his book *Capitalism, Socialism, and Democracy,* Schumpeter maintains that the eventual fall of capitalism will be due not to its inefficiency or to the exploitation of the masses, as Marx would claim, but, on the contrary, to its high level of efficiency, which will ultimately undermine its socio-political base. Belloc's suggestion that the ideal capitalist attempts to produce goods so efficiently as to undermine his base of possible consumers (see pp. 99–101 of the present edition) is reminiscent of this suggestion.

Belloc's strident critique of capitalism did not make him a friend of "socialism," which he denounces pointedly: it restricts the freedom and independence of the individual and the family, and attacks the very concept of private property which is – in its Catholic sense – the very foundation of such freedom and independence. Without these, men and women simply become dependent upon the whims of the State. The lessons of twentieth-century history confirm this judgment more than amply, for the keynote of the "People's State" in the East and of the Welfare State in the West has been abject dependency.

Thus Belloc says that Catholics and those possessed of common sense and normal desires must seek to re-establish the Distributist State, which he defines as "a state of society in which the families composing it are, in a determining number, the owners of the land and the means of production as well as themselves the human agents of production (that is, the people who by their human energy produce wealth with those means of production)." It is, he writes, "probably the oldest, and certainly the most commonly found of all states of society."

Some readers may be disappointed that the present work lacks discussion of the practicality or even the possibility of establishing a Distributist system in our present society, or even in the society of Belloc's day. For a discussion of practicalities, readers can turn to his *Essay on the Restoration of Property*. What Belloc is calling for is admittedly a highly idealistic objective, difficult to put into effect in our contemporary society where political and economic life is vastly bureaucratized and exceedingly centralized. This was already the case in the early part of last century, perhaps explaining why Belloc did not live to see his objectives realized.

While *Economics for Helen* neither is nor was intended to be *the* greatest and most developed text on economics, it makes a significant contribution towards helping the reading public to come to a better understanding of economics by providing them with a brief, general summary of some of its fundamental principles.

In my view, most worthwhile in *Economics for Helen* is Belloc's advocacy of Distributism insofar as it opposes the slow erosion of personal freedoms and the ever-widening power of the omnipotent state. Future generations must credit Belloc with being one of the few intellectuals who saw these dangers at such an early stage. These dangers plague us still; so if Belloc were ever relevant, he has never been so more than now; and if the world has ever needed the brilliance and clarity of Belloc's thought, it has never been more so than now.

Alberto Piedra, Ph.D.
Professor Emeritus of Economics
Catholic University
December 8, 2004
Feast of the Immaculate Conception
of the Blessed Virgin Mary

INTRODUCTION

WHEN *Economics for Helen* first appeared, it was reviewed in two of the leading economics journals of the day.[1] Although one review was not wholly negative, neither were overly sympathetic to Belloc's treatment of economics. While some of the strikes these reviewers made against *Economics for Helen* are accurate, speaking strictly from a modern and technical standpoint, they nevertheless demonstrate a profound lack of effort and imagination on the part of the reviewers to try to understand Belloc's project. Indeed, they reveal much more about the prejudices and predilections of the reviewers than they do about the alleged deficiencies of Belloc's system of thought. These reviews are not atypical but rather are symptomatic of the rough treatment Belloc has received at the hands of his critics. The professional reception to Belloc's ideas has ranged from benign neglect all the way to vigorous theoretical interpolation and reinterpretation. Indeed, there has been a sustained effort to recast Belloc's *The Servile State* as a precursor to Friedrich Hayek's *The Road to Serfdom* and to spin Belloc as a capitalist apologist. Yet these attempts to shoehorn Belloc's economics into a classical liberal mold fail to take account of the full breadth and novelty of his ideas.

With respect to Belloc's reviewers, a question such as, "What animates Belloc such that he would go to the trouble of writing a popular treatment of economics?" is never asked. Questions about the coherence, cogency, scale, and scope of his intellectual project are never addressed because to ask such questions would mean that Belloc's arguments must be taken seriously and not dismissed out of hand. The driving force behind these reviews seems to be a *desire to debunk* rather than to understand Belloc's concerns. These reviews are evidence of the profession's uneasy relationship with "outsiders" who dare write about economics and consequently are often labeled as "cranks." Yet Belloc displays neither the hubris nor the invincible ignorance of an economic "crank." Rather he adopts the stance of

---

[1] J. E. LeRossignol, *The American Economic Review,* Vol. 15, No. 1 (March, 1925), pp. 84–85; and H. Reynard, *The Economic Journal,* Vol. 34, No. 136 (December, 1924), pp. 620–621.

one who recognizes that economics does have something important to teach us, and that we would be wise to listen.

Yet one must wonder: "Why all the hostility?" Perhaps to the reviewers Belloc's work appeared dated and obscure; *dated* because of his reliance on classical economic concepts and *obscure* because of his penchant for inventing idiosyncratic terminology. True, there are times when neither Belloc's popular language is as precise nor his exposition as careful as one would like. Yet surely it would be a pity to be denied the views of so lively a literary imagination. It is well to keep in mind that *Economics for Helen* is a "popular" book, not a professional treatise. And notwithstanding its "amateur" nature, when its views are compared with those of Belloc's contemporaries, they are by no means farfetched, and indeed some of them are downright prescient. For example, while many saw socialism as *the* solution to the economic and social troubles of the day, Belloc saw it, with its accompanying state planning, for what it truly was.

Economics for Helen draws on the classical school of economics, explaining economics by intuitive metaphor and relying on real world examples. The point was not to serve up a dish only for economists; Belloc knew that economics was far too important to be left solely to the specialists. Critics confuse Belloc's desire to write for a popular audience, and to eschew the trappings of the professional economist, with ignorance. A lack of mathematics does not mean a lack of a model. Neither does it mean a lack of relevance or intellectual coherence. Surely Belloc's works such as *The Servile State* will be remembered long after the work of his critics has been forgotten.

Economics for Helen provides the economic foundation for Belloc's political and social thought. It reveals Belloc to have been a systematic thinker whose views on social organization emanate from his political economy. Once one has mastered *Economics for Helen*, his other works such as *The Servile State* and *The Restoration of Property* can be seen as part of the same intellectual project. It is fortuitous, therefore, that IHS Press has chosen to reissue *Economics for Helen*, for it may well lead to a renewed interest in Belloc's thought.

Belloc's Classical Origins

Belloc's treatment of economics follows a venerable tradition. A modern economist may well be put off by Belloc's "classical" analysis, having but a dim notion of what the classical school was all about. He might even believe that this is a decided handicap to Belloc's entire enterprise, relegating his slim volume to the dustbin of history. Yet, our modern-day economist would be much too hasty. As for the classical school that informs his work, for Belloc economics is much more than just supply and demand. Economics is the study of wealth, and political economy is the political application of economic science to the problem of scarcity in the face of human fallibility and sin.

Belloc say that the purpose of economics must be properly understood:

> The Science of Economics does not deal with true happiness nor even with well-being in material things. It deals with a strictly limited field of what is called "Economic Wealth," and if it goes outside its own boundaries it goes wrong. Making people as happy as possible is much more than Economics can pretend to. Economics cannot even tell you how to make people well-to-do in material things (p. 35).

Nevertheless, Belloc contends, economics is of use because "it can tell you how exchangeable Wealth is produced and what happens to it; and as it can tell you this, it is a useful servant."

From this perspective economics is a tool; a means to an end but not the end itself. As Belloc is quick to note, the science of economics itself is not about "true happiness" or about right and wrong, but rather it is a means by which we understand how the world works. With this knowledge of how exchangeable wealth is produced, "economic science," properly understood, under moral guidance, is a tool that can be used to produce human happiness.

Belloc's economics makes a number of distinctions that were part of the classical canon but which overtime fell by the wayside (though this neglect does not in any way invalidate those distinctions). For example, Belloc relies on the classical distinction between value in exchange and value in use. A horse may be of great usefulness to us, Belloc notes, but that is distinct from what the horse will fetch in the market place, and it is not the task of economics to explain "use value." Rather economics explains the value of the horse in exchange and how it will vary with market conditions. *Economics,* for Belloc, *explains how these values in exchange are created.*

Belloc is careful to distinguish between the market valuation of a good and the happiness it produces. Something may aid in the production of wealth yet have little ability to make us happy; something may have little exchange value yet yield a great deal of human happiness:

> A thing may be of the highest temporal use to humanity in the production of happiness, such as good singing, or of high spiritual value, such as good conduct, and yet that thing must not be confounded with economic values. When one says, for instance, that good singing, or a good picture, or a good book has no economic value, or only a very slight material economic value (the best picture ever painted has probably not a true economic value of more than 20s. outside its frame, unless the painter used expensive paints or a quite enormous canvas) one does not mean, as too many foolish people imagine, that therefore one ought not to have good singing, or good pictures, or the rest of it (p. 170).

Economics may explain why diamonds are dear and water cheap, but that in no way means that diamonds have a higher use value than water. Since "Economic wealth is a separate thing from well-being," then it may well be the case that "economic wealth [is] increasing though the general well-being of the people is going down," or "it may increase though the general well-being of the people around it is stationary" (p. 35).

With a proper understanding of economics we will not confuse an increase in wealth with a rise in economic well-being or happiness. Thus armed, we will be able to consider the *political application of economics* knowing that to do so we must also "consider human happiness, which is the object of all human living..." (p. 92).

Control of the Means of Production

For Belloc the central issue of social organization is *control*. Whosoever controls the means of production determines whether the society is socialist, capitalist, or distributist, and this control will not only have an effect on how much a society produces but will have an effect on the kinds of institutions, norms, and, yes, even people that society "produces." The economics of his day *abstracted* from these effects since, as Paul Samuelson wrote in 1957, "in a perfectly competitive market it really doesn't matter who hires whom: so let labor hire 'capital.'"[2] Within neo-classical economic theory it is pretended that capital's command and control over labor is of no social conse-

---

[2] "Wages and Interests: A Modern Dissection of Marxian Economics," *American*

quence, and that labor could just as easily employ capital. Almost a decade later, this view was eloquently summed up by Lionel Robbins who defined economics as the study of the allocation of scarce resources among competing alternatives. This reduces economics to mere social engineering, in which economic exchange is imagined to be an already "solved political problem."

For the classical economists though, it made a difference who hired whom, and for Belloc it does too. For Belloc, as a student of classical economics, the classical conceptions of land, labor, and capital played a significant role in how he framed and interpreted economic problems. Indeed Belloc's emphasis on the importance of *ownership* and *control* of the means of production was an example of his "empirical realism" in action. An understanding of the real way in which the world works, coupled with an experience of its working, served to temper the impulse to deal only in the abstract. Political and moral choices not only had to be economically viable but also realizable, given the present state of the world. Belloc certainly believed that we should do something to improve society; but he was at the same time a realist because he insisted that institutions must take into account human psychology and human longings. If our analysis leaves this out, he thought, then it is deficient.

Belloc considers four different societies in this book, defined in terms of ownership and control of the means of production. For Belloc there are "only three actual states of which we know anything in history and can deal with as real human experiences...the Servile State, the Capitalist State, and the Distributive State." Interestingly Belloc relegates the socialist alternative to the realm of the unknown precisely because it is a state about which we know nothing in history and of which we have no "human experience."

Yet at the time of *Economics for Helen,* many advocates touted the "benefits" of just such a society. Belloc, the realist, was not persuaded by socialist appeals to emotion. He was wary of such an all-encompassing system that had not yet met the test of the *real* world. Some have tried to portray Belloc as a utopian, promoting an untried and untested alternative to capitalism known as Distributism. It is true that Belloc was an avid advocate of Distributism, yet the notion that he was a utopian, and not a realist, is very far from the truth. Belloc makes it clear in *Economics for Helen* that how a theory works out in practice is important for determining whether one's economics is in accord with the real world. Indeed, when there are a lot of [first principles, both economic and non-economic] at work...they may modify the effect in practice to any extent. When people object to "theoretical dreaming" as they call it, they mean the bad habit of thinking that one conclusion from one particular set of first principles is sufficient and will apply to any set of circumstances. It never does. One has always to watch the thing in practice, and see what other forces come in" (p. 81).

Belloc goes to great lengths in his writings to provide the historical case for Distributism. One may seek to find fault in his scholarship, yet one may not find fault with his legitimate use of the tools he had at hand to demonstrate his case. Looking to actual existing historical episodes is just as "scientific" when controlled experiments are not readily available. In fact, his analysis of the Middle Ages relies precisely on that, a natural experiment that must be judged as either a success or failure but certainly not dismissed out of hand as "unscientific."

Belloc separates positive economics, or what he calls "scientific economics," from the value judgments we make about economic outcomes or the political application of economics. In the economics profession this separation has led to a sharp distinction made between facts and values. A number of economists have concluded that since people disagree about fundamental moral questions, reasoned argument cannot settle such disputes. And so it is with higher and lower preferences, according to this point of view. Given the professional predisposition of economists, preferences are treated as given and no distinction is made between higher and lower pleasures. Yet the classical economists made this distinction. They recognized that it is relevant economically. They argued that high pleasures required reason and often meant the active, painful pursuit of knowledge. They not only saw people as pursuing goods, but they also saw the preferences with which people appreciated them. This constitutive view of exchange means that our desire to acquire our preferences may well be hindered by firms that cater to vices and a society characterized by an overemphasis on the accumulation of money. With a few exceptions, textbook economics has been largely critical of such views. Yet for Belloc the "modern" economist's distinction between "is" and "ought" does not imply all views are equally plausible or acceptable and therefore deserving of equal weight. Belloc is rather on the side of the classical economists, and he takes this distinction to mean that if we are to act responsibly, our moral judgments must take into account the laws of economics.

Belloc and "Free Market" Capitalism

Because of this awareness Belloc avoids two tempting but erroneous claims sometimes made in defense of free market capitalism. The "productivist" view of income distribution claims that the combination of free markets and competition will ensure that we receive what we produce. The "just deserts" view claims that markets and competition will deliver an income that reflects what we deserve. *Neither claim follows from positive economics.* Hence, Belloc argues that with respect to "Rent" or "Interest":

> It does not follow because Rent or Interest are present that such and such rich men, or the State, or the labourers, have a right to them. *That is for the moralist to decide;* and men can in such matters make what arrangements they will. All economic science can tell us is how to distinguish between the three divisions, and to remember that they are inevitable and necessary (p. 58). (emphasis mine)

Unlike some prominent economists of his day, Belloc does not make the error of assuming that the market outcome is *necessarily* the moral one. It may well be morally repugnant and require intervention. Neither does this mean that anything goes. We must temper the application of our moral desires by the realities of the world.

> The only difficulty is to keep in our minds a clear distinction between what is called economic law, that is, the necessary results of producing wealth, and the moral law, that is the matter of right and wrong in the distribution and use of wealth.
>
> Some people are so shocked by the fact that economic law is different from moral law that they try to deny economic law. Others are so annoyed by this lack of logic that they fall into the other error of thinking that economic law can override moral law (p. 47).

Belloc was careful to separate the science of economics – the study of wealth creation – from the political application of the principles of economics. At the same time, Belloc's interest was not solely to "explain why an egg costs more than a cup of tea," as Joan Robinson derisively described the preoccupation of a large number of her fellow economists. Instead, Belloc wished to apply economics to improve the human condition: "political applications of political economy [require that we] consider human happiness, the whole purpose for human living." Economists who do not do so shirk their duty to humanity and "fall into the other error of thinking that economic law can override moral law."

Belloc's study of wealth creation, and the role that exchange plays in it, led him to view markets in an expansive sense. For Belloc the term "market" referred to an entire constellation of economic relations. Some commentators have erroneously associated Belloc with the classical liberal tradition that tends to stress the accountability role that markets play, over their distributional role. Yet this tends to downplay Belloc's recognition of the constitutive nature of market exchanges and the power relationships that are involved. Emblematic of Belloc's classical roots, he tended to separate distribution and production. For Belloc the distribution of income was not determined by the laws of economics but instead was subject to "the customs of society, or laws." Once output is produced, society plays a role in how it is distributed. However, there are restrictions on the ability of a society to affect its income distribution. Changes in the distribution of income can have disincentive effects that lead to a reduction in output. Belloc's Distributism shares an affinity with Mill's vision of a society that could alter the natural order of production by exercising its moral will.

Yet it is remarkable that Belloc was thinking in terms of a *proprietary economy*, while the economics of Belloc's day was characterized by a stale debate between a "command" and a "market" economy. From this perspective, the task of the politician is to find the appropriate mixture of command and competition. In this case markets are perceived merely to allocate resources and distribute income. Yet, as Belloc makes clear, markets do something much more – they give rise to various forms of human development. *Some institutions are more compatible with human nature and psychology than others.* Markets are much more than allocational mechanisms. Economists have a history of ignoring the extra-economic effects of "economic" choices and assuming that we must choose either command, competition or some combination of the two. This is in stark contrast to the economics of the classical school. Moral and cultural imperatives play an important role in a society's economic success, and the classical economists knew it! Belloc's use of the classical model, in which distributional issues are treated separately from issues of production, allows for consideration of *how* the surplus is distributed; this demonstrates that Belloc's view of economics informed his argument about the servile state. Hence Belloc's beliefs that a Distributist society is economically feasible and that capitalism, if left unchecked, will tend to evolve into the servile state are not *ad hoc* improvisations (as some of his critics would have it); they are rather consistent with, and indeed flow quite naturally from, his economics.

With respect to capitalism Belloc also places great emphasis on the bargaining position of the worker *vis à vis* the firm. The insecurity and material insufficiency facing the worker, engendered by capitalism, gives the employer power over the worker. Hence the centrality of "control" to his political economy. Striking a theme found in the works of both Adam Smith and Karl Marx, Belloc pointed ominously to the alienation and other human costs of wage labor organized under "capitalist" conditions. Despite their classical heritage, however, these extra-economic effects of markets were downplayed by post-classical economics

Compared with the classical approach, which makes room for the social effects of markets, the neo-classical model appears unduly restrictive. Textbook neo-classical theory routinely denies that markets are arenas of political power; and it in fact rejects the idea that markets are political.

The economist Abba Lerner aptly characterized this approach when he wrote, "An economic transaction is a solved political problem. Economics has gained the title 'queen of the social sciences' by choosing *solved* political problems as its domain." Yet Belloc's work has focused on precisely the fact that political and economic problems affect each other; what to do politically is, for Belloc, very much of an open question, and one which is intimately interrelated to questions of economics. *One domain is not isolated from the other.*

Belloc takes it as a given that labor markets do not "clear" (where a "clearing" market is one in which both sides balance out so that none remain who wish to transact but cannot, i.e., none remain unemployed), and although he does not offer an analysis of why that is the case (in terms that would satisfy a modern economist), nevertheless as an empirical observation, with respect to the labor markets of his day, it is a more-than-adequate working hypothesis. Belloc notes that employer bargaining power over the worker does exist, and that it is not inconsequential. For the neo-classical economists of the time, the markets did not clear (i.e., there was unemployment) because wages were too high, not because of difficulties inherent to the modern labor problem.

Markets shape and mold the rules of the game, i.e., the system of property rights. But do markets do a good job of this in the sense of providing rules that are fair or even efficient? Economic theory provides no reason to believe that markets can lead to efficient rules, let alone fairness, and Belloc concurs: "a great many people try to get out of what it is their duty to do politically by pleading that Economic Law prevents it" (p. 78). Or, as he says further,

> Many men take refuge in the excuse that, with the best will in the world, they cannot work such and such a social reform because economic science prevents their doing what they know to be right. If we know our Economics properly we can refute these false arguments, to the great advantage of our own souls and of our fellow-men.
>
> For instance: it is clearly our duty today to alleviate the fearful poverty in which most Englishmen live. A great many people who ought to know better say, or pretend, that economic laws prevent our doing this act of justice. Economic laws have no such effect; and an understanding of Economics clears us in this matter, as we shall see later on" (p. 80).

Indeed there is every incentive for agents that exercise power to shape and mold the rules so as to benefit them, leading to what Belloc called an oligarchy of the wealthy. Hence Belloc's account of markets stressed their inherently political nature, and capitalism for Belloc gave rise to relationships of dominance and subordination. To thwart these tendencies he made the case for widespread ownership of property. This argument not only rests on the economic rationale of altering the incentive structures in the economy to improve the well-being of the population (which is *the* fundamental reason for studying economics), but it also represents the expression of Belloc's deeply held democratic views emanating from his Catholic beliefs. Christianity teaches that we are all of us equal in the eyes of God. Indeed, in this sense, Distributism is putting Christian teaching into practice. Distributism *is* democracy via economic means. Democratic theory holds that those who enter into relationships involving power should have a say over how that power is exercised. Thus, democratic grounds for the regulation of this power relationship do exist and Belloc takes it as a given that the capitalist-worker relationship is just such a relationship.

Belloc sees dependency as degrading, humiliating, and dehumanizing. According to Belloc, we should all applaud whenever a person's sense of control over his own life is expanded. Whenever a person derives pleasure and security from his own resources, his self-esteem increases. From Belloc's viewpoint, dependency is a tragedy forced upon the working class due to "a hard bargain"; it is *not* a result of a rational choice. A change in the economic order that reduced the dependency, the precariousness, and material insufficiency of the working classes would be a welcome improvement.

Defenders of free markets have claimed that markets ensure that parties to an exchange are accountable and reduce the power others may exercise. Markets are accountable in the sense that consumers vote with their dollars and with their feet. Firms that perform according to the expectations of consumers will prosper, and firms that do not will fail the market test. Thus markets are accountable in the sense that someone theoretically has the ability to exit from a particular market transaction, seeking an exchange elsewhere. This accountability mechanism is in contradistinction to the mechanism of democracy that gives an equal *voice* to all. Consumers, participating in the accountability model, may express their preferences by their "dollar votes," but not all preferences carry equal weight. Those with greater income have more dollar votes to cast. Voice, on the other hand, means that agents can have a say in how they are governed. Distributism is an attempt to strengthen the roles of exit *and* voice. Distributism aims to make agents sufficiently well-off so that they need not enter transactions that they deem unfavorable, and to encourage and foster the growth of co-operative institutions, such as democratic firms and guilds, while at the same time retaining the accountability which markets afford. Belloc was well aware of the potential benefits of exchange and understood that the benefits of market exchange could well be lost if exchanges were improperly regulated. Indeed, this was a central aspect of his attack on Socialism.

Belloc's Critique of Socialism

When Belloc turns his analytical guns on Socialism nothing remains standing. Employing an argument with a long and respected pedigree, Belloc's evaluation of Socialism relied on a fundamental objection. "Men are not angels," Belloc observed, echoing a tradition in political economy whose modern incarnation goes back at least as far as Hume. This seemingly innocuous assumption has borne much fruit, playing a key role in the rise of the public choice school of economics, and even yielding a Nobel Prize. Socialism, in effect, gets all of the incentives wrong. Given that people are fallible and tend to pursue their own interests once in power, they will seek to satisfy their own needs and desires rather than those of others. There are parallels between this hypothesis and the Christian concept of fallen man. Scholars have noted that classical economics has some degree of affinity with Christian doctrine, and that this affinity has played a role in the 19th century anti-slavery coalition of economists and Christians.

Given that "men are not angels," Belloc's second objection followed: the accountability mechanism of the market would be severely hampered, if not non-existent, under Socialism. Writing in the latter half of the 1930s, Belloc observed that Russia was run solely for the benefit of "Stalin and his friends." Agents no longer have opportunities to exercise choice. The power to choose – what economists call "consumer sovereignty" – is greatly diminished.

Third, the psychology of most people is not compatible with life under Socialism. Here the claim is that it does not in fact take men as they are. Although he notes that a change in the system of distribution and allocation, as well as ownership and control, will lead to a society creating different people, nevertheless the bulk of people when it comes to ownership and control *need to express themselves*. The Left has often reminded us that a society should permit people to become the authors of their own lives to a reasonable degree. That is a good in and of itself. Property ownership is natural to people, and to have anything less is to reduce their status to that of children. Under Socialism the vast majority would be "children" with the state as guide and caretaker.

This leads to a forth point. For Socialism to be consistent with human psychology it would require some kind of state religion, or an ethos that would amount to a state religion. People are willing to sacrifice in a time of great need, such as wartime, and are willing to defer gratification today in the hope of having greater pleasure tomorrow. To pursue the goals of the state people must be willing to "have the material side of their lives administered for them" to such a degree that they are willing to live the life of a secular monastic. Yet it is not realistic to ask this of everyone, since it will not be forthcoming except by *force*.

Fifth, the very people who would be asked to run such a great state apparatus would be the ones who were successfully chosen by the political process. The very people, Belloc argues, "coveting public office" and living "the life of intrigue necessary to get it" would not be likely to be so unselfish as to be devoted to this new communal ideal (see p. 109 of the present edition).

Sixth, it would require the sacrifice of not merely a part of one's freedom but rather all of it. "There would be no way out." The necessity of the complete control of the individual was surely a prescient foresight on Belloc's part, and it is witness to his blending of an economic critique based on incentives and the psychology of people as people. Such state control – the necessary conclusion of State Socialism – would be stultifying and morally repugnant.

Belloc is skeptical that the "theoretical dream" of Socialism, once confronted by the actualities of the real world, would ever long take hold. Thus for Belloc Socialism is only possible under a unique set of circumstances: self-forgetfulness, completely other-regarding preferences, and complete submission of will to authority – which sounds remarkably like the requirements for life in a monastery.

The Upshot of Belloc's View

What are we to make of Belloc's arguments that capitalism is inherently unstable, that socialism and capitalism are not long-run solutions, that capitalism tends to evolve into the servile state, and that our only solution is Distributism? From the perspective of his contemporaries, Belloc's analysis is striking and authoritative. Writing before the ascendancy of the welfare state, Belloc sees the growing power of large firms, taking over the duty of providing security for the workers to ensure that there will be no work stoppages. His warning about a society dominated by large firms coupled with a waning of workers' desire for freedom and independence should strike us as prescient. As a social critic Belloc is undervalued; his accurate predictions at once put to shame the heady expectations of the Fabians, who thought that capitalism would slowly be eliminated by piecemeal legislation.

The Bellocian prognosis about the collapse of capitalism or the return of the servile state was a possible future path; although it was an unsettling vision, nonetheless, as Belloc argued, it was not meant to be gloomy, but factual. There is no denying his prescience when he spoke of the growth of the strength and size of business, for we have witnessed the rise of the multinational, lumbering giants, who know no borders, and contend for shares in world markets.

Belloc was also right in foreseeing a dramatic change in social relations, but what he did not see concretely (and perhaps could not have seen) was how those social forces would actually play themselves out: from the rise of the welfare state, the increasing strength of the laboring classes *vis à vis* the corporate firms, legal advances extending and protecting the rights of workers, and the phenomenal economic growth in the West. From the perspective of the post-world war baby boom period, the growth records of the world economies were nothing short of spectacular. In that light Belloc's warnings of the encroaching servile state and the instability of capitalism perhaps seems to be wide of the mark. Yet Belloc's themes of capitalist instability and personal insecurity have not left us; they have merely changed their *forms*.

Looking over just the last twenty years of world economic performance, one can only marvel at the tumult and unease that shook capitalist institutions to their foundations. Policy makers who had proclaimed that the troubles of capitalism were a story fit only for the history books had visited upon them scenes (Enron, Worldcom, Parmalat, and others) reminiscent of Belloc's era, as financial crises and panics spread from Asia to South America. It is precisely in this vein that Belloc noted that capitalism is unstable. If anything, he merely underestimated the ability of the capitalist system to respond and to shore up its defenses: that is to say, he underestimated the determination and ingenuity of those who strive to maintain economic power.

That system will not, though, be able to put off the inevitable reckoning forever. It is for this reason that the IHS Press release of a new edition of *Economics for Helen* is most timely, for today we must answer precisely the same questions, and face that same problems, that confronted Belloc.

Edward A. McPhail, Ph.D.
Assistant Professor of Economics
Dickinson College, Pennsylvania
December 28, 2004
Feast of the Holy Innocents

PREFACE

"Stephen Roach, the chief economist at investment banking
giant Morgan Stanley [says that] America has no better than a 10
percent chance of avoiding economic 'Armageddon.'"

—Brett Arends, *BostonHerald.com*, November 23, 2004

DISTRIBUTISTS like Hilaire Belloc are often accused of being
"dreamers," who look backwards to a time when men possessed
productive property that, with their own labor, could produce real
property in turn. No doubt *Economics for Helen*, the Distributist "Intro
to Economics," will also be dismissed as "unrealistic," for it bases its
economic principles and formulae upon tangible realities. Property is
firstly a field, a cow, a tractor, a loom, a lathe; and only secondarily (if
ever) a bond, a mortgage, a derivative, or a Federal Reserve Note.

If this seems quaint in light of modern perceptions, it would be
well to look at what so-called "reality" is today. Lest we too perhaps
scoff at Belloc's notions – for instance, that wealth is the exchange
value that attaches to a *thing*, that the "Distributive state is the natural
state of mankind," that currency must be "stable in value," and that fiat
money is "one of the very worst things that has happened" – we should
compare his "dreaming" with the profound and dangerous *unreality* of
economic life as it is lead in this third millennium A.D.

Much would be required to detail the fiction of "modern economics," worse even in practice than in theory. Simple common sense,
though, reveals the silliness of what today's economy is about. Is it necessary that basic tools and consumables be manufactured thousands of
miles from where they will be used and consumed? Should it be that
for Americans to become home "owners" they must pay money back
to a lender two, three, or four times over, when the lender did *no work*
and sacrificed *no capital* to loan the money into existence? Is it the case
(using Chesterton's example) that milk should come out of a "clean
shop" and not a "dirty cow;" and that the average American dinner
should travel 1500 miles before being consumed? Are things "normal"
in the "world's breadbasket" when we've lost 5 million family farms
since 1930, only 1% of Americans still live on a farm (compared to

50% a half-century ago), 62% of our agricultural output is produced by just 3% of our farms, 42% of produce is retailed by only *five* different concerns, 71% of government subsidies to keep the system running went (over the last 7 years) to only 10% of the farms, and farmers are only getting *9 cents* worth of every dollar spent on food, while the rest goes to suppliers, processors, middlemen, and marketers?

If this is "reality," then let us have a healthy dose of Belloc's "quaint" vision of real land, real food, real products, and real people!

***

The insanity doesn't stop here. All of the above is the result of what Bob Precher, writing recently for *The Daily Reckoning*, has termed the "credit-bubble" that has been "70 years in the making." The bulletin's editors note "the rise of consumer-credit capitalism [in which] people switched their attention from assets to cash flow... from balance sheets to monthly operating statements...from long-term wealth building to paycheck-to-paycheck financing...from saving to spending...and from 'just in case' to 'just in time.'" Many sneered at Belloc's prediction that capitalism would break down of its own accord, but these observations in fact imply that, absent the creation of huge volumes of credit, the breakdown would have occurred long ago.

At any rate, the inevitable cannot be put off indefinitely, even with credit. It may be (though no one can say for sure) that the chickens of finance-capitalism are now coming home to roost. Let's consider how.

First, there is *U.S. Government debt*. Two years ago, when IHS Press's edition of Belloc's *Essay on the Restoration of Property* was released, Uncle Sam was in debt by $6.12 trillion. America's treasurers left that figure in the dust on November 18, 2004, passing a limit-increase to $8.18 trillion. Morgan Stanley's chief economist, Stephen S. Roach, said that this "open-ended license for...fiscal irresponsibility is a recipe for disaster." Congressman Ron Paul, a Republican from Texas, called it "a disgrace," noting that the requirement for Congress to approve increasing the national debt ceiling used to cause members some embarrassment and act as a break upon increasing America's arrears. Now it's "merely another technicality on the road to bankruptcy." With the Congressional Budget Office predicting that soon almost ten percent of the federal budget will be for interest payments, Paul's statement is hardly hyperbole.

Second is *mortgage debt*. This too has risen $2 trillion since our release of Belloc's *Restoration*. This "funny money" (funny to all but those in debt), rather than savings and real wealth, is what's keeping the economy running. As Richard Benson, president of the Specialty Finance Group, noted recently, the "increase in mortgage debt represents the spending that the Bush Administration needed to keep a $12 trillion economy moving forward." There's a bright spot: home "ownership" rose 2 percent to an all time record of 67.2! "The bad news," Benson says, "is what had to be done to get it there while the labor force participation rate has dropped 2 percent! ...[E]asy credit and record low interest rates have boosted home sales. In previous economic cycles, the boost...came from rising incomes and more jobs!" The home-sale fantasy doesn't end there. The engines that drive housing finance – the Government-Sponsored Enterprises Fannie Mae and Freddie Mac, that fund the process (with around $150 billion of government subsidy) by purchasing mortgages (providing more cash to lenders), bundling them, and selling them into a complex derivative "cash and carry" trade – are both under investigation for accounting irregularities that might impact earnings and losses by several billion dollars.

Third is *corporate debt*. Corporations being "in the hole" is not news; what is, though, is their increasing inability just to stay afloat. Beyond their total debt of some $7 trillion(!), major corporations can no longer keep up their end of the bargain as participants in the Servile State. Committed to caring for employees, cradle-to-grave, automakers and airlines find it impossible to meet their pension commitments. Doing so puts them further in debt, until the "realists" admit the process is unsustainable. Thus US Airways refused to continue making pension-plan payments, declaring at a recent bankruptcy filing: "It would be 'irrational' to make pension contributions" (as Jim Jubak, an *MSN Money* editor, reported) "because 'it provides no benefit to the estate.'" Delta pilots, faced with the same eventuality, "opted to pull the financial ripcord." The alternative, Jubak explained, is for "senior pilots [to file] for early retirement by the hundreds and then [take] their pension in a lump-sum payout." He summarized the upshot thus:

> Welcome to the bankruptcy economy, where companies and governments walk away from long-standing promises to workers, and where workers scramble to collect as much as they can now in fear that even less will be available tomorrow.
>
> Bankruptcy, either formally declared in the case of troubled companies or informal in the case of cities or the U.S. government, will restructure the entire economy in coming decades.

Fourth: *consumer debt.* In 2003 it was $1.98 trillion. Americans consume more than they can pay for. A paycheck is frequently spoken for by mortgage, school, and other payments, leaving the groceries to go "on the card." The assessment from Tamara Draut, a director at Demos, a public policy institute that looked into credit card debt recently, is not pretty. "Too many Americans are drowning in credit card debt as a way to deal with the rise in the cost of living as their incomes have stagnated or dropped. It's...the band-aid holding the family budget together...." With savings at their lowest level since 1959 (excluding the month following the September 11th attacks, when the savings rate went to *minus* 0.2%!), credit cards must pick up the slack. As Marshal Auerback's *International Perspective* reported, "the savings rate has averaged below 1% for the first nine months of 2004 – the first time this has happened in seven decades." How else, then, to keep consumption going than by credit?

Finally, *deficits.* Continuously adding to much of our debt, the deficits in America's budget and current account reflect another denial of reality: they presume a limitless ability to get more than we can pay for. While the budget was balanced until Bush 43 unbalanced it by nearly $500 billion, the current account – reflecting trade and other financial flows across American borders – remains in the red by $660 billion. A remarkable paper by Nouriel Roubini and Brad Sester calls this deficit "the defining feature of the global economy right now," pointing out that the U.S., "the world's largest economy – and the world's pre-eminent military and geo-strategic power – is also the world's largest debtor." This deficit also "looks set to expand significantly in 2005 and 2006," for our massive consumption of Asian-produced goods is not poised to decrease any time soon. With money flowing overseas and goods coming in, it's not *American* manufacturers, businesses, and laborers who are being remunerated. As James Gipson, manager of the ClipperFund, wrote in his shareholder letter: "A slowly and likely growing share of our output of goods and services will go to provide comfortable retirements for the residents of Tokyo, not Topeka."

To make up for money leaving the U.S., the Treasury must sell debt paper *to the tune of some $46 billion per month.* Jim Sinclair, a veteran commodities and foreign currency trader, notes how precarious this is: "It is not necessary for major nations to sell U.S. debt in order to un-float the boat of the U.S. dollar...not buying as significantly as before will do the exact same thing. As the inflow to the U.S. falls below $46 billion per month, the need per month rises, *and so begins the* *process of drowning in debt"* (emphasis ours). China's recent announcement "that it is considering the sale of U.S. dollar-denominated Federal Debt," coming on the heels of "Russia's decision to consider doing the same thing [to shift] to Euro-based items," means that the system could unravel sooner than many think.

***

Even a casual survey of the landscape reveals a desert of deficits, debt, and default. "Creative" financing has kept the system working where by all rights it should have failed long ago. Credit has made the penniless into consumers. Sale of government debt has covered the decline of manufactured exports and the irresponsibility of government accountants. "Bankruptcy" laws have swept corporate insolvency and incompetence under the rug. Factory-farm overproduction is subsidized even as it destroys the middle-class family farm. And the list goes on.

Fantastic (as in fantasy) finance is thus a "virtue" covering a multitude of sins. Critics forget this when saying Belloc erred in predicting capitalism's demise. With *total* debt over 400% of GDP, $48 trillion dollars worth (4 times GDP) of the economic wealth of our nation *still has to be paid for!* What use is the capitalist wealth-creation engine if it only *loans* things to us at compound interest? Though a few can make great sums of money with unreal financial tools that postpone the inevitable, it's of no use for those aspiring to be owners *of more than just debt.*

Fr. Denis Fahey's vision must be taken to heart: finance exists to facilitate production, and production to meet the material needs of man; it's that simple. Submission to that principle would initiate a "return to the real" (as Gustav Thibon put it), opposing the profound *unreality* of credit and money-breeding, so characteristic of modern economic life.

A few "professional" thinkers are coming to their senses. Denouncing the "new paradigm" – the so-called "miracle of international finance" – claimed by proponents of the debt and credit system, the above-cited Stephen Roach says candidly, "this is an insane way to run the world." Yet his comment does not mean that the common man is returning to his place as master of production and finance, for that return is opposed by those who master them now. Pius XI warned in 1931 that "no one can breathe against their will" (*Quadragesimo Anno,* §106). Today they maintain an even tighter grip, as detailed in John Perkins's book, *Confessions of an Economic Hitman.* The Bush administration's failure to warn Venezuelan President Hugo Chavez of the coup against him, and its sponsorship of the opposition in Venezuela's August, 2004, recall election (both punishment(?) for Chavez's demand

for a higher percentage of oil revenues and his land-redistribution pro-
gram favoring Venezuela's poor); and the forcible creation of what the
Economist called "a capitalist dream" in Iraq (at a current cost of almost
$210 billion – ironically, the predicted figure that cost Bush's economic
advisor his job!) – all lend a disturbing credibility to Perkins's thesis.

***

Economics for Helen, herewith presented again, offers a true (and
thus simple) sketch of economic principles to help at least our minds to
return to *reality*. We can then disconnect in practice too from the unreality of modern economic life, to recover the contact with nature and real
property that was once mankind's "natural state." Being *productive* will
then mean not conducting on-line stock trades, but growing vegetables,
learning a craft or trade, and mastering the basics of economic reality:
food, shelter, clothing. Where two or three families unite to pursue this
end, as many already have, there's no limit to what can be achieved.

Eventually, this personal and practical return must lead to a broad
re-evaluation of whether the "comfortable" life really means instant
coffee, three cars, a DVD player with surround-sound system, and a
microwave oven that predicts the weather. These gadgets have profound
social costs; some of them *may cost too much* if we want to escape the
unreal world of wage slavery, mass production, and debt speculation.

There are rough times ahead for credit- and finance-capitalism.
Observant pundits are now predicting *de*flation from an inevitable
interest-rate hike as the Asians lose interest in bankrolling the dollar;
this in turn means possible "depression." Belloc said that "things will not
get right again...until society becomes as simple as it used to be," and on
that way *back to reality* there will no doubt be suffering: "We shall have
to go through a pretty bad time before we get back to that." Let us not
fear, however; if the future brings suffering, it will also bring wisdom,
even about things economic. Meanwhile, we must have the sense to look
and plan ahead, seeking out and acting upon wisdom where it can be
found. Belloc's *Economics for Helen* is a fine place to start.

The Directors
January 2, 2005
Feast of the Holy Name of Jesus

INTRODUCTORY NOTE

ECONOMICS is the name which people have come to give to the study of Wealth. It is the study by which we learn how Wealth is produced, how it is consumed, how it is distributed among people, and so on. It is a very important kind of study, because it often depends upon our being right or wrong in Economics whether we make the whole State poorer or richer, and whether we make the people living in the State happier or not.

Now as Economics is the study of Wealth, the first thing we have to make certain of is, *What Wealth is.*

"The Distributive State is the natural state of mankind. Men are happiest in such conditions; they can fulfil their being best and are most perfectly themselves when they are owners and free."

PART I

The Elements

I

WHAT IS WEALTH?

The Economic definition of WEALTH is subtle and difficult to appreciate, but it is absolutely essential to our study to get it clear at the outset and keep it firmly in mind. It is through some muddlement in this original definition of Wealth that nearly all mistakes in Economics are made.

First, we must be clear as to what Wealth is *not*.

Wealth is never properly defined, for the purposes of economic study, by any one of the answers a person would naturally give offhand. For instance, most people would say that a man's wealth was the money he was worth. But that, of course, is nonsense; for even if there were no money used his possessions would still be there, and if he had a house and cattle and horses the mere fact that money was not being used where he lived would not make him any worse off.

Another and better, but still a wrong, answer is: "Wealth is what a man possesses."

For instance, in the case of this farmer, his house and his stock and his furniture and implements are what we call his "wealth." In ordinary talk that answer will do well enough. But it will not do for the strict science of Economics, for it is not accurate.

For consider a particular case. Part of this man's wealth is, you say, a certain grey horse. But if you look closely at your definition and make it rigidly accurate, you will find that *it is not the horse itself which constitutes his wealth, but something attaching to the horse,* some quality or circumstance which affects the horse and gives the horse what is called its VALUE. It is this *value* which is wealth, not the horse. To see how true this is consider how the value changes while the horse remains the same.

On such and such a date any neighbour would have given the owner of the horse from 20 to 25 sacks of wheat for it, or, say, 10 sheep, or 50 loads of cut wood. But suppose there comes a great mortality among horses, so that very few are left. There is an eager desire to get hold of those that survive in order that the work may be done on the farms. Then the neighbours will be willing to give the owner of the horse much more than 20 or 25 sacks of wheat for it. They may offer as much as 50 sacks, or 20 sheep, or 100 loads of wood. Yet the horse is exactly the same horse it was before. The wealth of the master has increased. His horse, as we say, is "worth more." *It is this* WORTH, *that is, this ability to get other wealth in exchange, which constitutes true Economic Wealth.*

I have told you that the idea is very difficult to seize, and that you will find the hardest part of the study here, at the beginning. There is no way of making it plainer. One has no choice but to master the idea and make oneself familiar with it, difficult as it is. WEALTH *does not reside in the objects we possess, but in the economic values attaching to those objects.*

We talk of a man's wealth or a nation's wealth, or the wealth of the whole world, and we think at once, of course, of a lot of material things: houses and ships, and pictures and furniture, and food and all the rest of it. But the Economic Wealth which it is our business to study is not identical with those *things*. Wealth is the sum total of the *values* attaching to those things.

That is the first and most important point.

Here is the second: WEALTH, for the purposes of economic study, *is confined to those values attaching to material objects through the action of man, which values can be exchanged for other values.*

I will explain what that sentence means.

Here is a mountain country where there are few people and plenty of water everywhere. That water does not form part of the economic *wealth* of anyone living there. Everyone is the better off for the water, but no one has *wealth* in it. The water they have is absolutely necessary to life, but no man will give anything for it because any man can get it for himself. It has no *value in exchange*. But in a town to which water has to be brought at great expense of effort, and where the amount is limited, it acquires a value in exchange, that is, people cannot get it without offering something for it. That is why we say that in a modern town water forms part of *economic wealth*, while in the country it usually does not.

We must carefully note that Wealth thus defined is NOT the same thing as well-being. The mixing up of these two separate things – well-being and Economic Wealth – has given rise to half the errors in Economic Science. People confuse the word "Wealth" with the idea of well-being. They say: "Surely a man is better off with plenty of water than with little, and therefore conditions under which he can get plenty of water for nothing are conditions under which he has *more wealth* than when he has to pay for it. He has more *wealth* when he gets the water free than he has when he has to pay for it."

It is not so. Economic Wealth is a separate thing from well-being. Economic Wealth may well be increasing though the general well-being of the people is going down. It may increase though the general well-being of the people around it is stationary.

The Science of Economics does not deal with true happiness nor even with well-being in material things. It deals with a strictly limited field of what is called "Economic Wealth," and if it goes outside its own boundaries it goes wrong. Making people as happy as possible is much more than Economics can pretend to. Economics cannot even tell you how to make people well-to-do in material things. But it can tell you how exchangeable Wealth is produced and what happens to it; and as it can tell you this, it is a useful servant.

That is the second difficult point at the very beginning of our study. *Economic Wealth consists in* EXCHANGEABLE *values, and nothing else.*

We must be as clear on this second point as we have made ourselves upon the first, or we shall not make any progress in Economics. They are both of them unfamiliar ideas, and one has to go over them many times before one really grasps them. But they are absolutely essential to this science.

Let us sum up this first, elementary, part of our subject, and put it in the shortest terms we can find – what are called "Formulae," which means short and exact definitions, such as can be learnt by heart and retained permanently.

We write down, then, two Formulae:

1. WEALTH IS MADE UP, NOT OF THINGS, BUT OF ECONOMIC VALUES ATTACHING TO THINGS.

2. WEALTH, FOR THE PURPOSES OF ECONOMIC STUDY, MEANS ONLY EXCHANGE VALUES: THAT IS, VALUES AGAINST WHICH OTHER VALUES WILL BE GIVEN IN EXCHANGE.

II

THE THREE THINGS NECESSARY
TO THE PRODUCTION OF WEALTH –
LAND, LABOUR AND CAPITAL

YOU will notice that all about you living beings are occupied in changing the things around them from a condition where they are *less* to a condition where they are *more* useful to themselves.

Man is a living being, and he is doing this kind of thing all the time. If he were not he could not live.

He draws air into his lungs, taking it from a condition where it does him no good to a condition where it keeps him alive. He sows seed; he brings food from a distance; he cooks it for his eating. To give himself shelter from the weather he moulds bricks out of clay and puts them together into houses. To get himself warmth he cuts down wood and brings it to his hearth, or he sinks a shaft and gets coal out of the earth, and so on.

Man is perpetually changing the things around him from a condition in which they are *less* useful to him into a condition where they are *more* useful to him.

Whenever a man does that he is said to be creating, and adding to, Human Wealth: part of which is Economic Wealth, that is, Wealth suitable for study under the science of Economics.

Wealth, therefore, that thing the nature and growth of which we are about to study, is, so far as man is concerned, the result of this process of changing things to man's use, and it is through looking closely at the nature of this process that we get to understand what is necessary to it, and what impedes it, and how its results are distributed among mankind.

We must next go on to think out *how* Wealth is so produced. We have already seen what the general statement on this is: Wealth is produced by man's consciously transforming things around him to his own uses; and though not everything so transformed has true *Economic Wealth* attaching to it (for instance, breathing in air does not produce Economic Wealth), yet all Economic Wealth is produced as *part* of this general process.

Now when we come to examine the Production of Wealth, we shall find that *three* great separate forces come into it; and these we shall find to be called conveniently "Land," "Labour" and "Capital."

Let us take a particular case of the production of Economic Wealth and see how it goes forward. Let us take the case of the production of, say, 100 sacks of wheat.

1. LAND

A man finds himself possessed of so much land, and when he sets out to produce the 100 sacks of wheat, the following are the conditions before him.

There are natural forces of which he takes advantage and without which he could not grow wheat. The soil he has to do with has a certain fertility, there is enough rainfall to make the seeds sprout, and so on.

All these natural forces are obviously necessary to him. Though we talk of man "creating" Wealth he does not really create anything. What he does is to use and combine certain natural forces of which he is aware. He has found out that wheat will sprout if it is put into the ground at a particular season, and that he will get his best result by preparing the ground in a particular manner, etc. These natural forces are the foundation of the whole affair.

For the sake of shortness we call all this bundle of natural forces (which are the very first essential to the making of Wealth) LAND. This word "Land" is only a conventional term in Economics, meant to include a vast number of things beside the soil: things which are not Land at all; for instance, water power and wind power, the fertility of seed, the force of electricity, and thousands of other natural energies. But we must have some short convenient term for this set of things, and the term "Land" having become the conventional term in Economic Science for all natural forces, it is now the useful and short word always used for them as a whole: the reason being, I suppose, that land, or soil, is the first natural requisite for food – the most important of man's requirements, and the *place* from which he uses all other natural forces.

We say, then, that for the production of Wealth the first thing you need is the natural forces of the world, or Land.

2. Labour

But we next note that this possession of natural forces, our knowledge of how they will work, and our power of combining them, *is not enough to produce Wealth.*

If the farmer were to stand still, satisfied with his knowledge of the fertility of the soil, the quality of seed, and all the rest of it, he would have no harvest. He must, as we have said, prepare the land and sow the seed: only so will he get a harvest at the end of his work. These operations of human energy which end in his getting his harvest are called Labour: that is, *the application of human energy to natural forces.* There are no conditions whatsoever under which Wealth can be produced without natural forces or Land; but there are also no conditions whatsoever under which it can be produced without Labour, that is, the use of human energy. Even if a man were in such a position that he could get his food by picking it off the trees, there would still be the effort required of picking it. We say, therefore, that *all Wealth comes from the combination of Land and Labour:* that is, of *natural forces* and *human energy.*

3. Capital

At first sight it looks as though these two elements, Land and Labour, were all that was needed; and a very great deal of trouble has been caused in the world by people jumping to this conclusion without further examination.

But if we look closely into the matter we shall see that Land and Labour alone are *not* sufficient to the production of Wealth in any appreciable amount. The moment man begins to produce Wealth in any special fashion and to any appreciable extent, a third element comes in which is as rigorously necessary as the two others; and that third element is called Capital.

Let us see what this word "Capital" means.

Here is your farmer with all the requisite knowledge and the natural forces at his disposal. He has enough good land provided him to produce a harvest of 100 sacks of wheat if he is able and willing to apply his manual labour and intelligence to this land. But he must be kept alive during the many months required for the growth of the wheat. It is no use his beginning operations, therefore, unless he has a stock of food; for if he had not such a stock he would die before the harvest was gathered. Again, he must have seed. He must have enough seed to produce at the end of those months one hundred sacks of wheat. So we see that at the very least, for this particular case of production, the natural forces about him and his own energies would not be of the least use to the production of the harvest unless there were this third thing, a stock of wheat both for sowing and for eating.

But that is not all. He must be sheltered from the weather; he must be clothed and he must have a house, otherwise he would die before the harvest was gathered. Again, though he might grow a very little wheat by putting in what seed he could with his hands into a few suitable places in the soil, he could not get anything like the harvest he was working for unless he had special implements. He must prepare the land with a plough; so he must have a plough; and he must have horses to draw the plough; and those horses must be kept alive while they are working, until the next harvest comes in; so he must have a stock of oats to feed them with.

All this means quite a large accumulation of wealth before he can expect a good harvest: the wealth attaching to clothes, houses, food, ploughs, horses for a year.

In general, we find that man, when he is setting out on a particular piece of production of wealth, is absolutely compelled to add to his energies, and to the natural forces at his disposal, a third element consisting of *certain accumulations of wealth made in the past* – an accumulation of food, clothing, implements, etc. – without which the process of production could not be undertaken. *This accumulation of* ALREADY-MADE WEALTH, *which is thus absolutely necessary to production,* we call "Capital."

It includes *all kinds of wealth whatsoever which man uses* WITH THE OBJECT OF PRODUCING FURTHER WEALTH, *and without which the further wealth could not be produced.* It is a reserve without which the process of production is impossible. Later on we shall see how very important this fact is: for every healthy man has energy, and natural forces are open to all, but *capital* can sometimes be controlled by very few men. If they will not allow their capital to be used, wealth cannot be produced by the rest; therefore those who, by their labour, produce wealth may be driven to very hard conditions by the few owners of capital, whose leave is necessary for any wealth to be produced at all.

But all this we must leave to a later part of our study. For the moment what we have to get clearly into our heads are these three things: (1) natural forces, (2) human energy, and (3) accumulated stores and implements, which are called, generally, for the sake of shortness: "Land," "Labour," and "Capital." In the absence of any one of these three, production of wealth is impossible. All three must be present; and it is only the combination of all three which makes the process of producing economic values possible.

Points About Capital

There are *three* important things to remember about Capital.

1. The first is that what makes a particular piece of wealth into capital is not the kind of object to which the economic value attaches, but the *intention* of using it as capital on the part of the person who controls that object; that is, the intention to use it for the *production of future wealth.* Almost any object can be used as capital, but no object is capital, however suitable it be for that purpose, *unless there is the intention present of using it as capital.* For instance: One might think that a factory power engine was always capital. The economic values attaching to it, which make an engine worth what it is are nearly always used for the production of future wealth, and so we come to think of the engine as being necessarily capital simply because it is an engine, and the same is true of factory buildings and all other machinery and all tools, such as hammers and saws and so on.

But these things are not capital *in themselves;* for if we do not use them for the production of future wealth they cease to be capital. For instance, if you were to put the engine into a museum, or to keep a hammer in remembrance of someone and not use it, then it would not be capital.

And this truth works the other way about. At first sight you would say, for instance, that a diamond ring could not be capital: it is only a luxurious ornament. But if you use it to cut glass for mending a window it is capital for that purpose.

2. The second important thing to remember about Capital is that, being wealth, *it is at last consumed, as all other wealth is.* Capital is consumed in the process of using it to make more wealth, and as it is consumed it has to be replaced, or the process of production will break down. Take the case of the farmer we gave just now. He had to start, as we saw, with so much capital – horses and a plough and a stock of wheat and a stock of oats, etc.; and only by the use of this capital could he procure his harvest of 100 sacks of wheat at the end of the year; but if he is going on producing wheat year after year he must replace the wastage in his capital year after year. His stock of wheat for food and for seed will have disappeared in the year; so will his stock of hay and oats for keeping his horses. His plough will be somewhat worn and will need mending; and his horses, after a certain time, will grow old and will have to be replaced. Therefore, if production is to be continuous, that is, if there are to be harvests year after year, each harvest must be at least enough to replace all the wastage of capital which goes on during the process of production.

3. The third thing to remember about Capital is that Capital is *always the result of saving:* that is, the only way in which people can get capital is by doing without some immediate enjoyment of goods, and putting them by to use them up in creating wealth for the future. This ought to be self-evident; but people often forget it, because the person who *controls* the capital is very often quite a different person from the person who *really accumulated* it. The owner of the capital is very often a person who never thinks of saving. Nevertheless, the saving has been done by *someone* in the past, and saving must go on the whole time, for if it did not the capital could not come into existence, and could not be maintained once it was in existence.

Suppose, for instance, a man inherits £10,000 worth of capital invested in a Steamship Company.

This means that he has a share in a number of hulls, engines, stocks of coal and food, and clothing for the crews, and other things which have to be provided before the steamships can go to sea and create wealth by so doing.

All this capital has been saved by someone. Not by the man himself; he has merely inherited the wealth – but by someone.

Someone at some time, his father or whoever first got the capital together, must have forgone immediate enjoyment and put by wealth for future production, or the capital could not have come into existence. Thus, if the first accumulator of the capital had used his wealth for the purchase of a yacht in which to travel for his amusement, the labour and natural forces used in the production of that yacht would have made wealth consumed in immediate enjoyment, and it would not have been used for future production as is a cargo ship.

In the same way this capital, once it has come into existence in the shape of cargo ships and stocks of coal and the rest, would soon disappear if it were not perpetually replenished by further saving. The man who owns the shares in the Steamship Company does not consciously save year after year enough money to keep the capital at its original level.

Nevertheless, the saving is done for him. The Directors of the Company keep back out of the total receipts enough to repair the ships and to replenish the stocks of coal, etc., and they are thus perpetually accumulating fresh capital to replace the consumption of the old. How true it is that all Capital is the result of saving by *someone, somewhere,* we see in the difference between countries that do a lot of saving and countries that do little. Savages and people of a low civilisation differ in this very much from people of a high civilisation. They want to enjoy what they have the moment they have it, and they lay by as little as possible for the future; only just as much as will keep them going. But in a high civilisation people save capital more and more, and so are able to produce more and more wealth.

Now let us sum up in some more Formulae what we have learnt so far:—

1. ALL PRODUCTION OF WEALTH NEEDS THREE THINGS: (A) NATURAL FORCES, (B) HUMAN ENERGY, AND (C) AN ACCUMULATION OF WEALTH MADE IN THE PAST AND USED UP IN FUTURE PRODUCTION.

2. THESE THREE ARE CALLED, FOR SHORTNESS: (A) "LAND," (B) "LABOUR," (C) "CAPITAL."

3. THE LAST, CAPITAL, (A) DEPENDS FOR ITS CHARACTER ON THE INTENTION OF THE USER, (B) IS CONSUMED IN PRODUCTION, (C) IS ALWAYS THE RESULT OF SAVING.

III

THE PROCESS OF PRODUCTION

YOU have seen how the production of wealth takes place through the combination of these three things, Land, Labour and Capital, and you have also seen how the wealth so produced consists not in the objects themselves, but in the economic values attached to the objects.

Now we will take a particular instance of wealth and show how this works out in practice and what various forms the production of wealth takes.

Wealth, as we have seen, arises from the transposing of things around us from a condition where they are less to a condition where they are more useful to our needs.

Let us take a ton of coal lying a thousand feet down under the earth and no way provided of getting at it. A man possessing that ton of coal would not possess any wealth. The coal lying in the earth has no economic value attaching to it whatsoever. It has not yet entered the process whereby it ultimately satisfies a human need.

A shaft is sunk to get at that coal, and once the coal is reached a first economic value begins to attach to it. Next, further labour, capital and natural forces are applied to the task of hewing the coal out and raising it to the surface. This means that yet more economic values are attached to the ton of coal. These we express by saying that the ton of coal at the bottom of the mine, just hewed out, is worth so much – say 15/–; and later at the pit head is worth so much more – say £1. But the process of production of wealth is not yet completed. The coal is needed to warm you in your house, and your house is a long way from the pit head. It must be taken from the pit head to your house, and for this transport further labour, natural forces and capital must be used, and these add yet another economic value to the coal.

We express this by saying that the ton of coal *delivered* (that is, at your house) is worth not £1, which it was at the pit head, but £1 10s.; and in this example we see that transport is as much a part of the production of wealth as other work. We also see a further example of the truth originally stated that wealth does not consist in the object itself but in the values attached to it. The ton of coal is there in your cellar exactly the same (except that it is broken up) as it was when it lay a thousand feet under the earth with no way of getting to it. In your cellar it represents wealth. In possessing it you are possessing wealth to the amount of 30s. You could exchange it against 30s. worth of some other thing, such as wheat. But the wealth you thus possess is not the actual coal, but the values attaching to the coal. These economic values are being piled up from the very beginning of the process of production until the process of consumption begins.

Here is another case which shows how the process of production will add values to a thing without necessarily changing the thing itself.

Suppose an island where there is a lot of salt in mines near the surface, but with very poor pasture and very little of it; most of the soil barren and the climate bad. On the mainland, a day's journey from the island, there is good soil and pasture and a good climate, but there is no salt. Salt is a prime necessity of life, and it comes into a lot of things besides necessaries. To the people of the mainland, therefore, salt, which they lack, is of high value. To the people of the island it is of low value, for they can get as much of it as they want, with very little trouble. Meanwhile, meat is of very high value to the people of the island, who can grow little of it on their own soil, while it is of much less value to the people of the mainland, who have plenty of it through their good pastures and climate. Here we have, let us say, 100 tons of salt in the island and 100 tons of meat on the mainland. A boat takes the 100 tons of salt from the island to the mainland and brings back the meat from the mainland to the island. Here wealth has been created on both sides, although no change has taken place in the articles themselves except a change in position. Both parties, the islanders and the mainland people, are wealthier through the transaction, and this is a case where *exchange* is a direct creator of wealth, and the transport effecting the exchange is a creator of wealth.

Strictly speaking, everything done to increase the usefulness of an object right up to the moment when consumption begins is part of the production of wealth. For instance, wealth is being produced from the moment that wheat is sowed in the ground to the moment when the baked loaf is ready for eating, and the wealth expressed by the loaf, that is, the values attaching to it, are made up by all the processes of adding values from the first moment the seed was sown. When you eat a sixpenny loaf you are beginning to consume values created by the sowing of the wheat and its culture and its harvesting and grinding, and the working of the flour into dough, and the baking, and created by every piece of transport in the process, the carting of the sheaf into the rick, the carting of thrashed wheat to the mill, the taking of the flour to the baker, the taking of the baked loaf to your house, and even the bringing of the loaf from the larder to your table. Every one of these actions is part of the production of wealth.

There is attaching to the process of the production of wealth a certain character which we appreciate easily in some cases, but with much more difficulty in others. We have already come across it in discussing Capital. It is this:

All wealth is consumed.

This is universally true of all wealth whatsoever, though the rate of consumption is very different in different cases.

The purpose of nature is not the purpose of man. Man only creates wealth by a perpetual effort against the purpose of nature, and the moment his effort ceases nature tends to drag back man's creation from a condition where it is more to a condition where it is less useful to himself.

For some sorts of wealth the process is very rapid, as, for instance, in the consumption of fuel, or in the wasting of ice on a hot day. Man with an expenditure of his energy and brains applied to natural forces, and by the use of capital, has caused ice to be present under conditions where nature meant there to be no ice – a hot summer's day.

He has brought it from a high, cold place far away; or he has kept it from the winter onwards stored in an ice house which he had to make and to which he had to transport it; or he has made it with engine power. But the force of nature is always ready to melt the ice when man's effort ceases.

The moment man's effort ceases, deterioration, that is, *the consumption of the wealth present,* at once begins. And this truth applies at the other end of the scale. You may make a building of granite, but it will not last forever. The consumption is exceedingly slow, but it is there all the same. And whether the consumption takes place in the service of man (as when fuel is burnt on a hearth) or by neglect (as when a derelict house decays) it is always *economic consumption.*

We may sum up in the following Formulae:—

1. TRANSPORT AND EXCHANGE, QUITE AS MUCH AS ACTUAL WORK ON THE ORIGINAL MATERIAL, FORM PART OF THE PRODUCTION OF WEALTH.

2. ALL WEALTH IS ULTIMATELY CONSUMED: THAT IS, MATTER HAVING BEEN TRANSPOSED BY MAN FROM A CONDITION WHERE IT IS LESS TO A CONDITION WHERE IT IS MORE USEFUL TO HIMSELF, IS DRAGGED BACK FROM A CONDITION WHERE IT IS MORE TO A CONDITION WHERE IT IS LESS USEFUL TO HIMSELF.

IV

THE THREE PARTS INTO WHICH THE WEALTH PRODUCED NATURALLY DIVIDES ITSELF – RENT, INTEREST, SUBSISTENCE

W E now come to that part of Economics which has most effect upon human society, and the understanding of which is most essential to sound politics. It is not a difficult point to understand. The only difficulty is to keep in our minds a clear distinction between what is called Economic Law, that is, the necessary results of producing wealth, and the Moral Law, that is the matter of right and wrong in the distribution and use of wealth.

Some people are so shocked by the fact that Economic Law is different from Moral Law that they try to deny Economic Law. Others are so annoyed by this lack of logic that they fall into the other error of thinking that Economic Law can override Moral Law.

You have to be warned against both these errors before you begin to approach the subject of Rent, Profit and Subsistence. Only when we have worked out the principles of these three things can we come back again to the apparent clash between Economic Law and Moral Law, the understanding of which is so very important in England today.

The motive of production is to satisfy human needs, and the simplest case of production is that of a man working for himself and his family as a settler in a new country. He cuts down wood and brings it where it is wanted; he builds a hut and a bridge with it; he stacks it ready to burn for fuel. The wealth he thus produces by his labour goes to him and his, and because the labour he has to expend is what impresses him most about the process, he calls the wealth

produced at the end of it: "Wealth produced by his labour." He
thinks of his labour as the one agent of the whole affair, and so it is
the one immediate *human* agent; but, as we have seen, there are two
other agents as well. His mere labour (that is, the use of his brain and
his muscles) would not have produced a pennyworth of wealth, but
for two other agents: Natural Forces (or Land) and Capital. And we
shall find when we look into it that the wealth he thus produces and
regards as one thing is also really divided into three divisions: one
corresponding to each of the three agents which produce wealth.

Being a settler living by himself and possessing his own land
and his own implements, he controls all he produces and does not
notice the three divisions. But three divisions there are none the less
present in all wealth produced anywhere, *and these three divisions do
not correspond to the moral claim man has to the result of his labour.* They
are divisions produced by the working of Economic Law, which is as
blind and indifferent to right and wrong as are the ordinary forces
of nature about us.

These three divisions are called "Rent," "Interest" (or "Profit")
and "Subsistence." In order to see how these three divisions come
about we must take them in the order of *Subsistence* first, then *Interest*,
then *Rent*.

1. SUBSISTENCE

In any civilisation you will find a certain amount of things
which are regarded as necessaries. In any civilisation it is thought
that human beings must not be allowed to sink below a certain level,
and a certain amount of clothes of a certain pattern, a certain amount
of housing room and fuel, and a certain amount of food of a certain
kind are thought the very least upon which life can be conducted.
Even the poorest are not allowed to fall below that standard. This
does not mean that no one is allowed to starve or die of insufficient
warmth. It means that any particular civilisation (our own, for
instance, or the Chinese) has its regulation minimum and lets men
die rather than fall below it. This "certain amount," below which

even the poorest people's livelihood is not allowed to fall, is called THE STANDARD OF SUBSISTENCE.

Most people when they first think of these things imagine that there is some very small amount of necessaries which, all over the world, and at all times, would be thought absolutely essential to man. But it is not so. The standard set is always higher than the mere necessity of keeping alive would demand.

For instance, we in this country put into our standard of necessity clothes of a rather complicated pattern. We should not tolerate the poorest people going about in blankets. They must have boots on their feet, which take a lot of labour and material. We should not tolerate the poorest people going about barefooted, as they do in many other countries, nor even with sandals. It is not our custom. They may die of wet feet through bad leather boots and bad, thin clothing of our complicated pattern, but they must not wear wooden shoes or walk barefoot or go about in blankets.

Again, we do not live on anything at random, but upon cooked meat and a certain special kind of grain called wheat. There are some grains much cheaper than wheat; but our custom demands wheat even for the poorest, if there is not enough wheat there is a famine, and famine is preferred by society to the giving up of the wheat standard. Again, we insist upon even the poorest having a certain amount of protection against the weather in the way of houses, which must be up to a certain standard. We do not tolerate their living in holes in the ground or mud huts.

One way and another we have set up a certain Standard of Subsistence even for the poorest; *and every community in history has, at all times, lived under this idea of a* MINIMUM STANDARD OF SUBSISTENCE. This is so true that people will suffer great inconvenience, even to famine, as I have said, rather than give up the standard of subsistence. When people are too poor to afford this least amount of what we think necessaries effort is made to supply them by doles or a poor rate, or something of that kind; but the standard is not abandoned.

Well, this MINIMUM STANDARD OF SUBSISTENCE is the first division in the Wealth produced. The prosperous man, tilling his own land and possessed of his own capital, consumes, of course, much more than the bare standard of subsistence would allow. He eats more food and better food, and has more and better clothes and house room and fuel and the rest than the mere standard of subsistence of his civilisation demands. Nevertheless, even in his case the standard of subsistence is there. It is a minimum below which, if things went wrong, he would not fall. Ask him to fall below it and he would simply fail to do so. He would try to produce that minimum amount of wealth in some other way, or if he could not do that he would die.

This Standard of Subsistence, which is to be found in its various shapes in every civilisation, may be called "The Worth While of Labour." Human energy would not be forthcoming, the work would not get done, unless at the very least the person doing the work got this Standard of Subsistence. In England today it is *set* for a man and his family at something like 35s. to 40s. a week. One way and another, counting for allowance in rent and overtime and so on, even the poorest labourer gets that, and if he did not get it labour would stop. Our civilisation would run to famine and plague rather than go below this minimum.

Another way of putting it is this: Under the standard of subsistence in our civilisation in England a man must, on the average, produce something like £2 worth of economic values a week, otherwise it is not worth while living, not worth while going on.

I say "on the average." A great many people, of course, produce nothing. But there must be an average production of that amount to keep society going at all, merely in labour, that is, in human energy and brains. As a fact, of course, the average production is much higher. But it could not fall to *less* than this without the production of wealth gradually coming to an end.

It is very important to recognise this principle in Economics, for it is nearly always misunderstood, and it makes a great difference in our judgment of social problems. You often hear people speaking as though the subsistence of their fellows might fall to any level so long as they had so much weight of food and amount of warmth as would keep them alive. But it is not so. Every society has its own standard, and will rather have men emigrate or die than fall below it: and that standard is the basis of all production. *It must be satisfied or production ceases.*

2. INTEREST

Now, if this Worth While of Labour was all that had to be considered, things would be a great deal simpler than they are. Unfortunately, there is another "worth while" from which one cannot get away, and which makes the second division in the produce of wealth. This is the "Worth While of Capital": called "Profit" or "Interest."

We must be careful not to mix up "Interest on Money," that is, the word "interest" in its ordinary conversational use, with true economic interest. Interest on money does not really exist. It is either interest on *Real Capital* (machines, stores, etc.) for which the money is only a symbol, or else it is Usury, that is, the claiming of a profit which is not really there; and what Usury is exactly we shall see later on. The thing to remember here is that there is no such thing in Economic Science as Interest on Money.

We have seen that capital cannot come into existence unless somebody saves. We have also seen that since it is always being consumed and must be replaced, the saving has got to go on all the time, if the production of wealth (to which capital is necessary) is to continue.

Now, as you will see in a minute, capital cannot be accumulated without some motive. You only accumulate capital by doing without a pleasure which you might have at a certain moment, and putting it off to a future time. You go without the immediate enjoyment of your wealth in order to use it for producing further wealth. That means restraint and sacrifice.

But restraint and sacrifice require some motive. Why should a man, or a society, do without a present enjoyment if the sacrifice is not to be productive of future good?

What happens is this: A man says: "On my present capital I can produce so much wealth. If I accumulate more capital I shall, in the long run, have a larger income. I will therefore forgo my present pleasure. I will add to my capital and have more income in the future through my present self-restraint." Or again: "If I don't *keep up* my capital by continual saving to replace what is consumed in production I shall gradually get *less* income."

But here comes in a very important law of Economics called "The Law of Diminishing Returns." After a certain point, capital as it accumulates, does not produce a *corresponding* amount of extra wealth. It produces *some* more, but not as much in proportion. For instance, if you till a field thoroughly with the use of so many ploughs and horses and so on, you will get such and such a return. If you add a great deal more capital in the shape of food for more labourers and more tillage till you treat the land as a sort of garden, you produce more wealth from that field; but though you may have doubled your capital you will not have doubled your income. You will only have added to it, say, half as much again. If you were to double your capital again, making four times your original amount, using a lot more food for labourers and a lot more implements, you would again have a larger produce, probably, but perhaps only double your original amount: *Four* times the original amount of capital, and only *twice*, say, the old income.

So the process goes on; and in all forms of the production of wealth this formula applies, and is true: *The returns of increasing capital, so long as the method of production is not changed, get greater in amount, but less in proportion to the total capital employed.*

Men developing a certain section of natural forces get 10 percent on a small capital, perhaps 5 percent on a larger one; on a still larger one only 2½ percent, and so on, if they apply that capital to the *same section* of natural forces and in the *same manner.*

Well, this advantage which a man gets by adding to his capital at the expense of present enjoyment can be measured.

For instance, a man owning a farm and tilling it himself gets a harvest of 1,000 sacks of wheat. In order to get this result he must have capital at the beginning of every year – ploughs and horses, and sacks of grain and what not – worth altogether 10,000 sacks of wheat. His income, in wheat, is one-tenth of his capital. Every ten sacks of capital produces him an income of one sack a year. He says to himself: "If I were to plough the land more thoroughly and put on a lot more phosphates and slag and get new, improved machinery I might get another fifty sacks a year out of the land, but this new capital will have to be saved."

He carefully saves on every harvest, exchanging the wheat for the things he needs in the way of new capital, until, after a few years, the implements and the phosphates and slag and the rest on his land, and all his other capital is worth much more than it used to be.

Instead of being worth only *one* thousand sacks, his capital is now worth *two* thousand sacks, and he gets the reward for his putting by and doing without immediate enjoyment in the shape of a larger harvest. But though he has doubled his capital he has not doubled his income. Instead of the old income of 100 sacks of wheat he is now getting 150 sacks of wheat. Thus though his income is larger, the *proportion* of that income to the total capital is less. For 1,000 sacks of capital he got 100 sacks of wheat at harvest; but now for 2,000 sacks of capital he only gets 150 sacks at the harvest. Or (as we put it in modern language), his income is no longer 10 percent on his capital, but 7½ percent only. He has a larger income, but it is smaller in proportion to the capital invested.

Now, although the 2,000 of capital invested is thus bringing him in a smaller *proportion* of income than the old 1,000 did, he thinks it worth while: because he is at any rate getting more *income;* 150 sacks instead of only 100. But there must come a time when he will no longer think it worth while to go on saving. Supposing he finds, for instance, that after taking all the trouble to accumulate and apply to his land capital to the value of 10,000 sacks of wheat, he gets only 200 sacks, that is 2 percent annual reward for all this saving, he will not think it good enough, and he will stop saving. The point where he stops, the return below which he does not think it worth while to save, marks the *minimum profits of capital.* A man is delighted, of course, to have *more* profit than this if he can. But the point is, he will not take *less.* Rather than make less than a certain proportion of income to his capital he will stop saving, and spend all he has in immediate enjoyment.

It is this obvious truth which makes the second great division in the produce of wealth. You must, as we have seen, produce enough to keep labour going. That is, you must produce enough to satisfy the standard of subsistence in your society; *but you must also produce enough more to keep capital accumulating.* You must produce, over and above subsistence, whatever happens to be the amount of *profits* for which capital will accumulate in any particular society (with us, today, it is about 5 percent).

It is very important to observe that this second division, PROFIT, or INTEREST, must always be present, no matter how the capital is owned and controlled, no matter who gets the profit.

Some people have thought that if you were to take capital away from the rich men who now own most of it and to give it to the politicians to manage for everybody, this division, Profit, would disappear. But it is not so. The people who were managing the capital for the benefit of everybody would have to tell the electors that they could not have all the wealth produced to consume as they chose: a certain amount would have to be kept back, and people would only consent to have a certain amount kept back on condition that they got an advantage in the future as a reward of their immediate sacrifice. Even if you had a Despot at the head of the State who cared nothing for people's opinions, this division of profit would still be there; for it would be mere waste to accumulate capital at a heavy sacrifice to himself and his subjects, unless it produced a future reward.

If the Despot said, "This year you must do without *half* your usual amount of leisure and without *half* your usual amounts, pay *double* for your cinemas and for your beer, and all that in order to earn one hundredth more leisure and amusements next year," it would be found intolerable.

So it comes to this: there are always present in the process of production two agents, Capital and Labour, and each of these must have in one form or another its "Worth While," otherwise it won't go on. You must satisfy the "Worth While of Labour" and you must satisfy the "Worth While of Capital." If you do not, labour stops working and capital stops accumulating, and the whole business of production breaks down.

(Of course, we must be careful to distinguish between the case of a private man increasing his investments and the general increase of capital as applied to an unchanging area of natural forces. John Smith having £1,000 invested at 5 percent can save another £1,000 and another and many more, and still get 5 percent. But that is because he is saving and makes up for others wasting, or because his saving is so small a proportion of the total Capital of Society that it has no appreciable effect. But if the total Capital of Society be thus increased the Law of Diminishing Returns eventually comes into play.)

3. RENT

We arrive through this at the third division, RENT.

Under some circumstances the Worth While of Labour and the Worth While of Capital can just barely be earned, and no more. Under those circumstances production will take place, but under worse circumstances it will not.

For instance, where there is very light, sandy soil near a heath a man finds that by putting a thousand pounds of capital on to a hundred acres of land he can get his bare subsistence and £50 worth of produce over: 5 percent on his capital. It is worth his while to cultivate that land, just barely worth his while. He also possesses land on a still more sandy part over the boundary of the heath itself. He calculates that if he were laboriously to save another £1,000 and take in 100 acres of the new, worse land, he would make the bare subsistence of the labour employed upon it, but only £10 extra, that is, only 1 percent on his new capital. He would say: "This is not worth while," and the too-sandy bit of land would go uncultivated.

When the conditions are such that the capital and labour applied to them *just* get their worth while and no more, those conditions are said to be "on the margin of production," which means that they are the worst conditions under which men in a particular society will consent to produce wealth at all. Put them on conditions still worse, and they will not produce.

Now the existence of this Margin of Production creates the third division in Wealth, which is called RENT.

Rent is the surplus over and above the minimum required by labour and capital out of the total produce. (We must be careful, as we saw in the case of "Interest," not to confuse true economic Rent with

"Rent" in the conversational sense. Thus what is called "the rent" of a house is part of its true economic rent, but part of it interest on the accumulated or saved wealth, the *Capital* of its bricks and mortar and building.)

Take the case of a seam of coal, which at one end of its run crops out on the surface, a couple of miles on is only 1,000 feet below the surface, but dips down gradually until, within twenty miles, it is 10,000 feet below the surface.

Under the conditions of the society in which the coal is being mined, and in the state which the science of mining has reached, it is found that, at a depth of 5,000 feet, this seam is *just* worth while mining: that is, the capital which has to be accumulated for sinking the shafts and bringing the miners up and down from their work, and raising the coal to the surface, and providing subsistence for the miners at their work, *just barely* gets the profit below which it would not be worth while to use it.

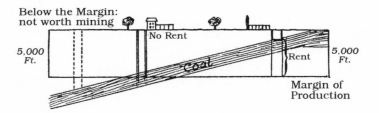

A shaft is sunk at this depth, for instance, and the machinery and stores cost £10,000, and when you get the coal to the surface that coal will pay the standard of subsistence of the labourers and leave £500 profit for capital; that is, 5 percent. Capital will not accumulate if it gets less than 5 percent. Labour will not be exercised if it gets less than its standard subsistence; therefore the coal which lies farther along the seam, deeper than 5,000 feet, will be left untouched. It is not "worth while" to sink a shaft to try and get it. It is "below the Margin of Production."

What happens to the coal in the places where it gets nearer and nearer to the surface? Obviously it is better worth while to sink shafts there than it is at 5,000 feet. You only want the same amount of labour for cutting the coal out, whether it is 5,000 feet below the surface or 2,000, and you want much less capital and labour in sinking the shafts and bringing the coal to the surface and getting the miners up and down. There is, therefore, a surplus. Thus with a shaft only 2,000 feet deep you need, say, only £5,000 worth of capital to get £500 worth of coal over and above the subsistence of the labourers. Five percent on £5,000 is £250 – so in that case there is a benefit of an extra £250 *after* the worth while of capital and labour are satisfied. Over and above what is just the worth while of capital and labour for getting the coal you have in the shallower mines extra value, and that extra value gets larger and larger as the distance of the coal from the surface gets less and less. The deepest mine is on what we call "the margin of production." It is just worth while to work it. The surplus values in all the shallower mines are called "Rent." If a landlord owned the coal in quite a shallow part where it was within a thousand feet of the surface, he could say to the labourers and the owners of capital who were coming to dig it out: "The mine which is working at 5,000 feet is just worth your while. If you work here at 1,000 feet you will have a great deal more than 5 percent on your capital, and the subsistence of labour is just the same. All this extra amount of values, however, I must have, otherwise you shall not work my coal."

Since the capitalists are content to accumulate capital for a return of 5 percent and the labourers to work for their subsistence, the extra amount is paid to the landlord. If one set of people refuse to pay it, there will always be another set of people who will be content to pay it and this extra amount or surplus is called "Economic RENT," which is something, of course, much more strictly defined than, and different from, what we call "Rent" in ordinary conversation.

Or again, take three farms of equal area but varying fertility. Each requires £1,000 capital to stock it and five labourers to work it. The £1,000 capital demands £50 a year profit. The five labourers need £500 in a year to meet their standard of subsistence. The poorest farm raises just £550 worth of produce a year. The next best raises £750, and the best one £950 worth. Then there is *no* economic rent on the first; it lies on the margin of production. There is £200 economic rent a year on the second, and £400 on the third.

We can sum the whole thing up and say that on the mass of all production there are three charges:

1. FIRST, THE CHARGE FOR THE SUBSISTENCE OF LABOUR.

2. NEXT, THE CHARGE OF PROFITS, OR INTEREST, FOR THE REWARD OF CAPITAL, THAT IS, OF SAVING, AND LASTLY

3. IN VARYING AMOUNTS, RISING FROM NOTHING AT THE MARGIN OF PRODUCTION, TO LARGER AND LARGER AMOUNTS UNDER MORE FAVOURABLE CIRCUMSTANCES, THE SURPLUS VALUE CALLED ECONOMIC RENT.

These three divisions are always present whenever wealth is produced. The same man may get all three at once, as happens when a farmer works good land which is his own. Or again, when one man owns the fertile land and another man provides the capital, and yet another man provides the labour, the three divisions appear as three incomes of Labourer, Farmer and Landlord receiving separately Wages, Profit and Rent. Whether these divisions appear openly, paid to different classes of men, or whether they are concealed by all coming into the same hands, they are present everywhere and always. That is a fixed economic law from which there is no getting away.

Always remember that these economic laws are in no way binding in a social sense. They are not laws like moral laws, which men are bound to obey. They are certain mathematical consequences of the very nature of wealth and its production, which men must take into account when they make their social arrangements. It does not follow because Rent or Interest are present that such and such rich men, or the State, or the labourers, have a right to them. That is for the moralist to decide; and men can in such matters make what arrangements they will. All Economic Science can tell us is how to distinguish between the three divisions, and to remember that they are inevitable and necessary. But we must wait until a little later on to discuss social rights and wrongs under Applied Economics and continue here for the present to confine ourselves to the Elements of Economic Law alone.

V

EXCHANGE

EXCHANGE is really only a form of production as we saw in the illustration of the island with salt and the mainland with meat. When the exchange of the things is of advantage to both parties it creates wealth for both, and profitable exchange is, therefore, when it takes place, only the last step in a general chain of production.

But Exchange is so separate an action that students of Economics have agreed to treat it as a sort of chapter by itself, and we will do so here.

The characteristic of Exchange is that you take a thing from a place where it has less value to a place where it has more value, thus adding an economic value to the thing moved and so creating wealth. In the same transaction you bring back something else against it, which has more value in your own place than it had in the place from which you took it, that is again adding an economic value and therefore creating wealth. We saw how this was in the case of the salt and the meat, and so it is with thousands upon thousands of exchanges going on all over the world.

For instance, we in England have grown fond of drinking tea in the last 200 years. But our climate will not allow us to grow tea. Tea can only grow in a very hot country.

Now in very hot countries specially heavy labour upon metal work is not be to expected. Men are not fit for it. But in this cool climate men are fit for it, and also men here have through long practice become very skilful at working metal: smelting iron, for instance, and making it up into machines.

Therefore, there is a double advantage to us and to the people who live in the hot countries where tea is grown if we *exchange*. We

send them metal things that we have made and which are useful to
them, and which they could hardly make themselves, or only with
very great difficulty (and, therefore, at a great expense of energy),
and we get from them tea, which we could not grow here except in
hot houses: that is, at much more expense of energy than is needed in
the countries where tea grows naturally out of doors.

When there are present two or more objects of this kind, such
that the exchange of them between two places will benefit both parties, we may speak of "a potential of exchange," stronger or weaker
according to the amount of mutual advantage derived.

This word "potential" you will not find yet in many books,
but it is coming in, for it is a very useful word. It is taken by way of
metaphor from Physical Science. When there is a head of water over
a dam, or a current of electricity of such and such an intensity, we talk
of the "potential" and measure it. For instance, we say this electrical
current is double the potential of that, or the head of water working
such and such turbines is at double the potential of another head of
water in the neighbourhood. In the same way we talk of a "potential"
of exchange, meaning a tendency for exchange to arise between two
places or people because it is of mutual benefit to both.

Potentials of exchange come into existence not only through
difference of climate or differences of habit, but also through what is
called the Differentiation of Employment, which is also called Division of Labour.

Thus two countries may be both equally able to produce, say,
metal work and silk fabrics, and yet if one of them concentrates on
getting better and better at metal work and the other on getting
better and better at silk fabrics, it may well be that both will benefit
by separating their jobs and exchanging the results. And this is true
not only of two countries, but of individuals and groups.

The cobbler does not make his own clothes. He makes boots,
and by learning his trade and getting used to it makes them much
better and in a much shorter time than other men could, and therefore makes a pair of boots with less expense of energy, that is, *cheaper,*
than another man would. The tailor can say the same thing about
making clothes. So it is to the advantage of the cobbler to exchange
his extra boots against the extra clothes the tailor has made.

In general: intelligent societies always tend to build up a very widespread system of exchange, because intelligent people tend to concentrate each on the job that suits him best, and also because intelligent people discover differences of climate and soil and the rest which may make exchange between two places a mutual advantage for both.

It is indeed a great mistake to do as some modern people do, and put Exchange in front of Production. Thus you hear people talking as though the trade a country does, the total amount of its exports and imports, were the test of its prosperity, whereas the real test of its prosperity is what it has the power to consume, not what it manages to exchange.

But still, though it comes at the end of Production and must never be made more important than the whole process of Production, Exchange is present universally wherever there is active production of wealth. Thus the group of people who build ships are really exchanging what they make against the produce of other people who make clothes and grow food and build houses, and the rest of it; and in a highly-civilised country like ours much the greater part of the wealth you see consumed around you has gone through many processes of exchange.

1. There are a few elementary Formulae concerning Exchange which it is important to remember.

THERE IS A POTENTIAL OF EXCHANGE, THAT IS, EXCHANGE TENDS TO TAKE PLACE, WHEN OF TWO OBJECTS THE PROPORTIONATE VALUES ARE DIFFERENT IN TWO DIFFERENT COMMUNITIES.

It is not very easy to understand the meaning of this until one is given an example. Supposing a ton of coal from England to be worth £2 by the time it is delivered in Cadiz, and supposing that making a dozen bottles of wine in England, with all the apparatus of hot-house grapes and the rest of it came to £5 of expense. Supposing that in Cadiz, from the small coal mines near by, they can produce coal at only £1 a ton, but on account of their climate they can produce a dozen of wine for a shilling. Then you get this curious situation:

It pays the exporting country, England, to sell coal in Cadiz *at less than its English economic value,* and to import the wine from Cadiz.

It pays your English owner of coal, although the values attaching to it by the time it has got to Cadiz are £2 a ton, to sell a ton of coal there for only £1, and to exchange that against the wine of Cadiz, and bring that back to England. At first sight it sounds absurd to say that selling thus at a lower value than the cost of production and transport can possibly be profitable. But if you will look at it closely you will see that it is so.

If the Englishman had tried to make his wine at home it would have cost him £100 to make twenty dozen bottles, but when he has sold his coal at Cadiz for £1 he can with that £1 buy twenty dozen of wine and bring it back to England. He is much the wealthier by the transaction, and so is the man at Cadiz. The Cadiz man could have spent his energies in digging out a ton of coal near Cadiz instead of importing it, but the same energies used in making wine produce enough wine to get him rather more coal from England.

2. The second Formula to remember about Exchange is this:

GOODS DO NOT DIRECTLY EXCHANGE ALWAYS ONE AGAINST THE OTHER, BUT USUALLY IN A MUCH MORE COMPLICATED WAY, BY WHAT MAY BE CALLED "MULTIPLE EXCHANGE."

Of course, the vehicle by which this is done is a currency, or *money*, which I will explain in a moment; but the point to seize here is that exchange is just as truly taking place when there is no direct barter of two things but a much longer and complicated process.

For instance, a group of people called a Railway Company in the Argentine want a locomotive. A locomotive can be produced cheaper and better, that is, with less expenditure of energy for the result, in England than in the Argentine. But on the other hand, England wants to import tea. Now the Argentine grows no tea. What happens? How does England get the tea? That locomotive goes out to the Argentine. An amount of wheat sufficient to exchange against the locomotive goes against it, *not* to England, but to Holland, a country which, like us, has to import a lot of wheat. As against the wheat sent to Holland, the people in Holland send, say, the cheeses which they make so well, on account of their special conditions, and the consignment goes to Germany. The Germans send out a number of rails equivalent to the number of cheeses and of the wheat and of the locomotive, as they are very good at making rails, and have specialised on it. But they do not send the rails to Holland. They send them to some Railway Company which has asked for them in Egypt. The Egyptian people send out an equivalent amount of cotton, which they can grow easily in their climate, and this cotton goes to mills in India, and against it there comes an equivalent amount of tea, but the tea does not go back to Egypt. It goes to England.

There you have a circle of Multiple Exchange in which everybody profits by the exchange going on, although it is indirect. In the same way, of course, it is true that all of our domestic exchanges at home are multiple. If I write a book which people want to read, whereas I want not books but several other things, boots and fuel and furniture, I do not take my books round to the man who provides boots and to the one who provides fuel and to the one who provides furniture. I go through the process of selling my book to a publisher, and through an instrument he gives me, called a cheque (I will explain this when we come to the point of money), I can obtain boots and fuel and furniture to the amount of the value of the books of mine which my publisher will sell. Yet when exchange is thus highly indirect and multiple it is just as much exchange as though I went and bartered one book for one pair of boots with the cobbler.

3. The third thing to remember about Exchange is of the utmost importance, because it has given rise to one of the biggest discussions of our English politics. The Formula runs thus:—

OTHER THINGS BEING EQUAL, THE GREATEST FREEDOM OF EXCHANGE IN ANY GIVEN AREA MAKES FOR THE GREATEST AMOUNT OF WEALTH IN THAT AREA.

It ought to be self-evident, but it is astonishing how muddled people get about it, when they become confused over details and cannot see the wood for the trees. It ought, I say, to be self-evident that if you leave exchange quite free, anybody being at liberty to produce what he can produce best, and exchange it for things which other men can produce better than he, both parties will tend to be the richer by such freedom and the wealth of the whole country will be greatest when all exchanges in it are thus left free to be worked by the sense of advantage.

If there were a law, for instance, preventing me from buying etchings, or preventing Jones, the etcher, from buying books, Jones would have to write his own books (or do without them, which is what he would do), and I should have to etch my own etchings, which would be exceedingly poor compared with the wonderful etchings of Jones. We are obviously both of us better off if we are left free to exchange what we can each make best. And so it is with all the countless things made in a State.

This principle applies not only to a particular nation but to the whole world. If you left the whole world free to exchange the whole world would be the richer for it. And any interference with exchange between one nation and another lessens the total possible amount of wealth there might be in the world.

So far so good; and, as I have said, such a truth ought to be self-evident. But here there comes in a misunderstanding of its application, and that misunderstanding has made any amount of trouble. It is so important that I must give it a separate division to itself.

VI

FREE TRADE AND PROTECTION

NATIONS, as we know, put up tariffs against goods which come from abroad: That is, their Governments tax imports of certain goods and thereby interfere with the freedom of exchange. For instance, the French have a tax of this kind upon wheat. Wheat grown in France will cost, let us say, £1 a sack, but the Argentine can send wheat to France at an expense of only 10s. a sack, because the land there is new, and for various other causes. If the wheat from the Argentine were allowed to come in freely, and the French to export against it things which they can make more easily than wheat they would have more wheat at a less total expense; but they prefer to put a tax of ten shillings upon every sack, that is, to put up a barrier against the import of wheat from abroad, and so keep up the price artificially at home.

When a nation does this with regard to any object that may be imported, if the object can also be produced within the nation (which it nearly always can) it is said to *protect* that object, and the system of so doing is called "Protection." The word arose from the demand of certain trades to be "protected" by their Governments without considering whether it was for the good of the whole nation or not. It obviously would be a very nice thing for people who breed sheep, for instance, in this country, if all mutton coming from the Colonies were taxed at the Ports, while the mutton grown inside the country were not taxed; for in this way the value of the mutton would rise in England, and the rise would benefit the sheep owners. But it would be at the expense of all the other people who did not grow sheep, and who would have to pay more for their mutton.

As opposed to this system of *Protection,* and interfering with international exchange by a tariff, intelligent people a long lifetime ago began to agitate for what they called "Free Trade," that is the putting of no tariff on to an import, or at least no tariff high enough to give an artificial price to the producer of the same thing at home. Thus, when England was completely Free Trading (which it was until the war) there was a tariff on tea; but that was not Protection, for those who would try to grow tea here would have to grow it in hot houses and at an enormous expense, and the tax on tea, though heavy, did not make it anything like so dear as to make it worth while to produce tea here.

Another principle of Free Trade was that if it was thought advisable to put a tariff on to anything coming into the country which could be produced in the country, then you would have to put what was called "an equivalent excise" on the thing produced at home. For instance, in order to get revenue, one might put a tax of a 1d. on the pound on sugar coming from Germany, but, according to the doctrine of Free Trade, you must put a similar excise (that is, a home tax of 1d. on the pound) upon any sugar produced in England. If you did not do that you would be benefiting the sugar manufacturer in England at the expense of all other Englishmen, which would be unjust and also make England less wealthy because it would be inducing Englishmen to make sugar by offering them a reward and so take them away from some production for which they were better fitted.

This idea, that Free Trade must necessarily be of advantage to everybody, and that it was only stupidity or private avarice which supported Protection, was very strong in England, and, in the form you have just read, it seems beyond contradiction.

But if you will look closely at Formula No. 3 written in the last division on page 63, you will see that there is a fallacy hidden in this universal Free Trade theory. It is perfectly true that free exchange over any area tends to make the wealth of all that area greater, and if the area include the whole world, then free exchange all over the whole world, that is, complete Free Trade, would make the world as a whole richer.

But it does not follow that EACH PART *of the area thus made richer is itself enriched.* That is the important point which the Free Trade people missed, and it is this which supports, in some cases, the argument for Protection.

If we allow free exchange everywhere throughout England, England as a whole will, of course, be the richer for it; but it is quite possible that Essex will be the poorer. If we allow Free Trade throughout all Europe, Europe will be the richer for it, but it is quite possible that some particular part of Europe, Italy or Spain, may be made poorer by the general process, and as they don't want to be poorer they will by Protection and tariffs cut themselves off from the area of free exchange.

THERE ARE CONDITIONS WHERE AN INTERFERENCE WITH FREE EXCHANGE OVER THE BOUNDARIES OF A PARTICULAR AREA MAKE THAT AREA RICHER: WHEN THOSE CONDITIONS EXIST, THERE IS WHAT IS CALLED AN ECONOMIC REASON FOR PROTECTION.

So we may sum up and say that the theory of universal Free Trade being of benefit to the world as a whole is perfectly true. If we are only considering the world, and do not mind what happens to some particular area of the world, then the case for Free Trade is absolute. But if we mind a hurt being done to some particular area, such as our own country, more than we mind the hurt done to the world as a whole, then we should look at our particular conditions and see whether our country may not be one of those parts which will be drained of wealth by Free Trade and will be benefited by artificially fostering internal exchanges.

In the second part of this book I will go into this again, and show how the discussion arose in England and what the arguments are for and against Universal Free Trade, and how true it is that a sound economic argument for Protection exists.

VII

MONEY

WHEN people begin exchanging by bartering goods one against another they at once find that there is an awkward obstruction to this kind of commerce; at least, they find it the moment there are more than two of them. It is this: that the person they are nearest to for the striking of a bargain may not want, at the moment, the particular thing they have to offer, but something else which a third party has who is *not* present.

For instance: John is a hunter who has a surplus of skins to offer. He can get skins easier than other people. William, farming good soil, has surplus wheat to offer, and Robert, living near a wood and skilled as a woodman, has extra wood to offer. John wants wood. He takes one of his furs to Robert and says: "I will give you this fur for a cartload of wood." But Robert may answer, "I don't happen to want a fur just now. What I do want is a sack of wheat."

Either no transaction will take place on account of this hitch, or one of these two things will happen: Robert will take the fur from John and give him his cartload of wood, and will then take the fur over to William, and see whether William wants a fur in exchange for some wheat. Or John, very much wanting the wood, will go to William, and if William wants a fur, will exchange it for wheat; then John will take the wheat back to Robert, and exchange it for the wood that he wants.

That is the sort of complicated and clumsy come-and-go that will be continually happening even with quite a few exchangers, and with quite a small number of articles. When it came to a great number of exchangers and a great number of articles the trouble would grow impossible and exchange would break down.

But things arrange themselves thus: It is soon found that one of the things which are being exchanged is easier to carry than the rest, and perhaps lasts longer and also can be easily used in small or large amounts. For instance, in the case of our three producers, John, William and Robert, *wheat* might easily appear in this character. People always want wheat sooner or later. It keeps well. It is not very difficult to transport, and you can divide it into quite small amounts, or lump it up in large amounts.

So the chances are that when any of the three wanted to benefit by getting rid of some of his surplus produce he would get into the habit of taking *wheat* in exchange, even if he did not want it for the moment. For he would say to himself: "I can always keep it by me and then exchange it against somebody else's produce when that somebody else happens to want wheat." Soon you would find each one of the three would be keeping a little wheat by him for the purpose of saving tiresome journeys to effect complicated double exchanges, and the wheat so used by all three of them would be in effect MONEY. It would be used as a common medium of exchange to facilitate the disposal of goods one against the other, without the elaborate business of making special barters, after long search.

Mankind has found, in most cases, that where a very large number of articles were being exchanged *two* in particular naturally lent themselves to this particular use, and those two were gold and silver. They have also used bronze, and even iron and in some places rare shells, and all sorts of other things. But gold and silver came to be for nearly all mankind, and are now for all civilised mankind, the objects which most naturally are used as money.

The reason for this is as follows:

The thing which naturally becomes money out of all the things that are exchanged will be that which best combines a certain number of qualities, some of which we have already mentioned, and of which here is a list.

1. It must be portable, that is, a large weight of it must take up little room, so that quite considerable values can be taken easily from place to place – for money has to be always moving from one to another to effect purchases and sales.

2. It must be easily divisible, for one is always wanting to use it in all sorts of amounts, very little and very large.

3. It must keep. That is, it must not deteriorate quickly, or it would have very little use as money.

4. It must be of an even quality, so that, wherever you come across it, you may count on its being pretty well always the same, and therefore weight for weight of the same value.

5. It must be more or less stable in value. It would be difficult to use as money some object which was very plentiful at one moment and suddenly scarce at another; very cheap this year, and very dear next year – such as are, for instance, agricultural products depending upon the season.

Now of all objects gold and silver best fulfil all these requirements. Precious stones are more portable, value for value. A £1,000 worth of diamonds takes up less space and is less heavy than a £1,000 worth of gold. And precious stones are fairly stable in value and also keep very well; but they are not easily divisible. Again, they are not of the same standard value in all cases. They vary in purity. But gold and silver have all the qualities required. Gold hardly decays at all through the passage of time, and silver very little; and each, but especially gold, is valuable for its bulk, and its value is fairly stable, and each is easily divisible and can therefore be presented in any amount, from a tenth of an ounce to a hundred pounds weight.

So, by the mere force of things, gold and silver became the money of mankind. People kept gold and silver by them in order to effect their exchanges, and very soon a producer did not feel himself to be exchanging at all (in the sense of exchanging goods against goods), but thought of the affair as "Buying and Selling." That is, of exchanging his produce, not against other produce, but against gold and silver, with the object of *later* re-exchanging that gold and silver for other things that he needed.

Money, once thus established, is called A MEDIUM OF EXCHANGE and also CURRENCY or THE CIRCULATING MEDIUM. It is called "currency" and "circulating" because it goes its round through society, effecting the exchanges, and this running around or circulating gives it its name: "That which is current" from the Latin for "running." That which "circulates" from the late Latin word for "going the rounds."

When gold and silver become the money of mankind it is important to be able to tell at once the exact amounts you are dealing with. This, under simple conditions, is done by weighing; but it is more convenient to stamp on separate bits of metal what weight there is in each, and that is called "coining the metal." All that a Government does when it makes a sovereign is to guarantee that there is so much weight of gold in the round disc of metal which it stamps.

Money does not only fill this main function of being a medium of exchange, that is, of making a vast quantity of complicated exchanges possible, it also has great social value as a measurer or standard, and soon after money comes into use men begin to think of the economic values of things in terms of money: that is, in what we call "Prices."

All things which men produce are fluctuating the whole time in value. There is now rather more of one article, and now rather less. A sack of barley at one moment will exchange exactly against a sack of wheat, and then in a few weeks against rather less than a sack of wheat. Meanwhile, where it used to fetch a lamb in exchange it may, in a few months, need two sacks for a lamb; and so with all the hundreds and thousands of other objects. When we have money the whole mass of transactions is referred to the current medium, and that is of immense social value. For no one could keep in his head all the changing exchange values of a multitude of articles one against the other, but it is easy to remember the exchange values against one standard commodity, such as gold. And whatever the exchange value is in gold we call the "price" of the article.

For instance, when you say that a house is worth £500, that is the "price" of the house, you mean that the amount of gold you would have to exchange to get it is about Ten Pounds weight of the metal. And when you say that the price of a ticket to Edinburgh is £4, you mean that the service of taking you to Edinburgh in the train will be exchanged against about an ounce of the metal gold.

I now come to a most difficult point about money and prices which is rather beyond the elements of Economics, but which it is important to have some idea of, though it is very difficult.

There is a very interesting study in Economics called "The Theory of Prices," showing why *all prices on the average* (what is called "General Prices," that is the value of all goods in *general* as measured against gold) sometimes begin to go up and at other times go down: Why goods as a whole begin to get dearer and dearer in gold money, or cheaper and cheaper. It is a complicated piece of study, and people dispute about it. But the general rules would seem to be something like this: the exchange value of things against gold, or the value of gold, against the things for which it exchanges (that is prices) is made up of two things: *First,* the amount of gold present to do the work of exchange; *Secondly,* the amount of work you can make it do in exchange: the pace at which you can get it to circulate. It is obvious that one piece of gold moving rapidly from hand to hand will do as much work in helping exchanges to be carried out as ten pieces moving ten times more slowly.

If, for any reason, the total amount of gold becomes suddenly smaller or suddenly larger, or if the pace at which it is used changes very quickly, then prices fluctuate violently.

Supposing you could, in a night, take away half the gold in circulation. Then, of course, the remaining gold would become much more valuable. In other words, prices would fall. For if an ounce of gold is rarer and more difficult to get than it was, it will exchange against, that is, "buy" more than it did; this means that "the price of things has fallen." We used to say, for instance, that a quarter of wheat was worth an ounce of gold. But if we suddenly change the amount of gold so that gold becomes much rarer and more valuable, perhaps an ounce of gold will buy not one quarter but two. The price of one quarter used to be an ounce of gold. Now the price is only half an ounce of gold. Wheat has become cheaper in proportion to gold, and "prices," that is, values measured in gold, in money, have fallen.

The same thing would happen if you did not lessen the amount of gold in circulation but made the circulation much more sluggish. The amount of gold in circulation would be the same, but as it went its rounds more slowly it would be more difficult to get a certain amount of gold in anyone place at any one time.

Prices, then, depend upon the actual amount of money that is present to do the work, *and* the pace at which it is made to go the rounds: or (to put it in technical terms), on the amount of the currency *and* its "efficiency in circulation."

Now, there is in the human mind a very strong tendency to keep prices stable. We think of them by a sort of natural illusion as though they were absolute fixed things. We think of a pound, and a shilling, and five pounds as real, permanent, unchanging values. If we find that quite suddenly five pounds will buy a great deal more than it used to, or quite suddenly a great deal less, if we are met by a sudden and violent fluctuation in prices of this kind, our minds tend, unconsciously, to bring things back, as much as possible, to the old position; and I will show you how this tendency works in practice.

Supposing a very great deal of gold, for some cause, were to disappear. People suddenly find prices falling very rapidly. A man with a £1,000 a year can buy twice as many things, perhaps, as he used to buy. On the other hand, a man with anything to sell can only get half the amount he used to get. For gold has become rarer, and therefore more valuable as against other things.

What is the result? *The result is a very rapid increase in the pace at which the gold circulates.* Every purchaser feels himself richer. The gold is tendered for a much larger number of bargains, and though the mind, by this illusion it has of gold value as a fixed thing, cannot bring the actual gold back, what it can do is so to increase the second factor, Efficiency in Circulation, as largely as to make up for the lack of gold; and under the effect of this prices will gradually rise again. In the same way, if the mass of current medium by some accident becomes suddenly increased that should lead to an equally sudden rise in prices; but the unconscious tendency of the human mind to keep prices stable sets to work at once. Efficiency in Circulation slows down, the new large amount of currency works more sluggishly, and, though prices rise, they do not rise nearly as much as the influx of money might warrant.

We see, therefore, that the factor in the making of prices called "Efficiency in Circulation" works like a sort of automatic governor, tending to keep prices fairly stable; but of course it cannot prevent the gradual changes, and sometimes it cannot prevent quite sharp changes, as we shall see a little later on. For the moment, the interesting thing to note about Efficiency in Circulation is that we owe to this factor in prices the creation of "Paper Money."

If, with only a certain stock of gold to work on, business rapidly and largely increases, if a great many more things are made and exchanged, then, as the gold will have a lot more work to do – and so become more difficult to obtain in any one time or place – that should have the effect, of course, of making it more valuable, that is, of lowering prices.

Now with the beginnings of modern industry, about a hundred and fifty years ago, a vastly greater number of things began to be made than had ever been made before, and the number of exchanges effected multiplied ten, twenty and a hundredfold. The stock of gold, though it was increased in the nineteenth century by discoveries in Australia and California, and later in South Africa, would have been quite unable to cope with this flood of new work, and prices would have fallen very much indeed, had it not been for the creation of Paper Money. Paper money was a method of immensely increasing Efficiency in Circulation.

This is how it worked.

A Bank or a Government (but especially the Bank of England, with the guarantee of the Government) would print pieces of paper with the words: "I promise to pay to the bearer of this Five Pounds." Anyone who took one of these pieces of paper to the Bank of England could get Five Golden Sovereigns. But since this was publicly known, people were willing to take the piece of paper *instead of* the five sovereigns.

If you sold a man a horse for fifty pounds, you were just as willing to take ten five pound notes from him as fifty sovereigns. They were more convenient to carry, and you knew that whenever you wanted the actual gold you had only to go to the bank and get it.

Because people were thus willing to be paid in paper instead of in the actual gold, a large number of notes could be kept in circulation at any one time, and only a small amount of gold had to be kept in readiness at the Bank to redeem them. In practice it was found that very much less gold than the notes stood for was quite enough to meet the notes as they were brought in for payment. Much the most of the note circulation went on going the rounds, and in normal times it took a long time for a note on the average to be brought back to the Bank.

You can see that this dodge of paper money had the effect of increasing the total *amount* of the current medium in practice, and of greatly increasing its Efficiency in Circulation. Moreover, it made the Efficiency in Circulation very elastic, because in times of quiet business, more notes would go out of circulation and be paid into the bank, while in time of active business more notes would go on circulating.

So long as every note was redeemed in gold every time it was brought to the bank, so long as the promise to pay was promptly kept, the money still remained good; the paper currency did not interfere with the reality of the gold values, there was no upsetting of prices, and all went well.

Unfortunately, Governments are under a great temptation, when they have exceptionally heavy expenses, to falsify the Currency. People get so much in the habit of trusting the Government stamp on paper or metal that they take it as part of nature. What the Government is really doing when it coins a sovereign is giving a guarantee that this little disc of yellow metal contains 123 grains of gold with a certain known (and small) amount of alloy to make the gold hard. When the Government has to pay a large amount in wages, or for its Army and Navy, or what not, it is tempted to put in less gold and more alloy and keep the old stamp unchanged, and that is called "Debasing the Currency."

For instance, the Government wants a hundred tons of wheat to feed soldiers with, and the price of wheat in gold at that moment is Ten Sovereigns a ton. It says to a merchant, "If you will give me a hundred tons of wheat, I will give you a thousand sovereigns." But when it comes to paying the thousand sovereigns, instead of giving a thousand coins with 123 grains of gold in each, it strikes a baser coin with only a hundred or less than a hundred grains in each, and pays the merchant with these. It is a simple form of cheating and always effective, because the merchant thinks the sovereign is genuine. Only when these bad sovereigns get into circulation they naturally find their level in gold; for people begin to test them, and find that they have not got as much gold in them as they pretend to have. Then, of course, prices as measured in this new base coin rise. If the Government wants to buy another hundred tons of wheat it must offer more than a thousand of the base coins; it must offer, say, thirteen hundred of them. But again it is tempted to put even less gold into the coins with which it pays for the second lot of wheat, and so the coin gets baser and baser, until at last, perhaps, a sovereign will not really be worth half what it pretends to be. Governments in the past have done this over and over again, but it was not until our time that the worst form of debasing the coinage came in.

It came in as a result of the Great War, and we are all suffering from it today. This last and worst form of debasing coinage worked, not through cheating about the metal, but through a trick played with paper money.

Before the war, if you got a Five Pound note saying "I promise to pay Five Pounds" the promise was kept and the five golden sovereigns were there for you whenever you went with your note to the bank and asked for them; but when the Government had these very heavy expenses to meet on account of the war, they first began making difficulties about paying when people brought their paper to the bank, and at last stopped paying altogether. At the same time, they did everything they could to get the gold out of private people's hands and to make them use paper money instead. The consequence was that, people being so accustomed to think of a paper guarantee of the Government exactly as though it were real money, readily took to the new notes and used them as money, thinking of these wretched bits of paper exactly as though they were so many golden sovereigns. The Government could go on printing as many bits of paper as it liked, and they would still be used as though they were real money. So long as the amount of paper printed was not more than *would have been printed* when the notes were redeemable, and when the currency was on a true "Gold Basis," no harm was done; but of course it paid the Government to go on printing a great many more notes than that, because, when it could make money thus cheaply, it could pay for anything, however great the expense; but at the cost, of course, of debasing the currency more and more.

This kind of money, forced upon people, pretending to be the same as real money but actually without a Gold Basis, is called "Fiat"† money, and that is the kind of money the whole world has

_____
† From the Latin word *Fiat*, "Let it be so." As though the Government had said:

today, except those countries which did not take part in the Great War, and the United States which did not ever give up its gold basis.

Of the different European fighting countries, however, ours did best in this matter. We are still living on Fiat money, and we have much more of it than we ought to have. But the French have more in proportion, so that prices measured in *their* money are now (1923) more than three times what they would be in gold. The Italians are worse off still. With them it is four times. With the Germans it is millions of times, and their currency has quite gone to pieces; a paper coin in Germany is worth (at the time I write, October, 1923) *ten million* times less than the real metal coin which it is supposed to represent.

This is one of the very worst things that has happened on account of the war, for as the money now being used all over Europe is not real money, no one feels certain whether he can get his debts really paid, or whether his savings are safe, or whether a contract made for a certain payment a few months hence will be really fulfilled or not. A man may lend a thousand francs or marks or pounds for a year, and then at the end of the year, when he is to be paid back, he may be paid in coin which has got so much worse that he is really receiving only half or a tenth or a thousandth of the real value he lent. A man in Germany sells a hundred sheep for so many marks, to be paid for in a month; and at the end of the month the marks will only buy ten sheep!

This piece of swindling, which has been the note of the last five years, is the first point we have touched on so far where a problem in Economics and the study of Economic Law brings one up against questions of right and wrong.

It is morally wrong for the Government to swindle people out of their property by making false money. What is the way out, allowing for Economic Law? It is morally wrong that some men should starve while other men have too much: allowing for Economic Law, what is the way out of such evils?

As you go on in the study of Economics you find quantities of questions where you have to decide whether economic laws

---

"This is not a piece of gold, only a piece of paper. But I say it is to be taken as gold. So I order. *Let it be so.*"

render possible political actions which you would very much like to undertake, and which seem right and just. Many such actions, though one would like to undertake them, cannot be undertaken because our study of Economics has shown us that the consequences will be very different from what we hoped.

On the other hand, a great many people try to get out of what it is their duty to do politically by pleading that Economic Law prevents it.

Before ending these notes, then, we must go into the main questions of this kind, and see what there is to be said, in the light of economic knowledge, for our present system of society, which is called CAPITALISM; for other systems in the past such as SLAVERY; for PRIVATE PROPERTY; for the various theories of SOCIALISM; for and against USURY, and so on.

It is necessary to go into these points even in the most elementary book on Economics, because the moment one begins the practical application of one's Economic Science these questions at once arise; to answer them rightly is the most important use we can make of economic knowledge.

PART II

POLITICAL APPLICATIONS

INTRODUCTION

So far I have been putting down the elements of Economics just as one might put down the elements of Arithmetic. But Economics have, just like Arithmetic, a *practical application:* if it were not for this, there would be no real use in studying Economics at all.

For instance: we find out, when we do the elements of Arithmetic, that solid bodies vary with the cube of their linear measurements. That is the general abstract principle; but the *use* of it is in real life when we come (for instance) to measuring boats. We learn there from Arithmetic that, with boats of similar shape, a boat twice as long as another will be eight times as big; it is also by using the elements of Arithmetic that we can keep household accounts and do all the rest of our work.

It is precisely the same with Economics. We are perpetually coming upon political problems which Economics illustrate and to which Economic Science furnishes the answer – or part of the answer – and that is where the theoretical elements of Economics have practical importance.

For instance: once we know the elementary economic principle that rent is a surplus, we appreciate that it does not enter into cost of production. We do not try to make things cheaper by compulsorily lowering rent. Or, again, when we have learned the nature of money we can appreciate the dangers that come from using false money.

In these political applications of Economics we also come upon what is much more important than mere politics, and that is the question of right and wrong. We see that such and such a thing ought to be so as a matter of justice; but we may blunder, as many great reformers have blundered, in trying to do the right thing and failing to do it, because we have not made a proper application of our Economic Science. And the opposite is also true: that is, a knowledge of Economics prevents their being wrongly applied by those who desire evil. Many men take refuge in the excuse that, with the best will in the world, they cannot work such and such a social reform because Economic Science prevents their doing what they know to be right. If we know our Economics properly we can refute these false arguments, to the great advantage of our own souls and of our fellow-men.

For instance: it is clearly our duty today to alleviate the fearful poverty in which most Englishmen live. A great many people who ought to know better say, or pretend, that economic laws prevent our doing this act of justice. Economic laws have no such effect; and an understanding of Economics clears us in this matter, as we shall see later on.

We have hitherto been following the statement and examination of economic laws: that is, the *theoretical* part of our study and its necessary foundation. Now we go on to the *practical* part, or "Applied Economics," which is the effect of those laws on the lives of men.

Before leaving this Introduction I think it is important to get quite clear the difference between what is called "theoretical" study and the practical application of such study. People are very often muddle-headed about this, and the more clearly we think about it the better.

A theoretical statement is a statement following necessarily and logically from some one or more known first principles. Thus, we know that two sides of a triangle are longer than the third, so we say it follows *theoretically* that a straight road from London to Brighton is quicker motoring than going round by Lewes. But the number of first principles at work in the actual world is indefinitely large. Therefore one must test any one theoretical conclusion by practice: by seeing how it works. Because, side by side with the one or two first principles upon which our theory is built, there are an indefinitely large number of other first principles which come into play in the real world. Thus there is, in motoring, the principle that speed varies with road surface. So the way round by Lewes may be quicker than the straight road if it has a better surface. There is yet another principle that speed is checked by turnings in the road, and it may prove that on trial the two ways are about equal.

Or again: we know that the tidal wave is raised on either side of the earth, and that there is, therefore, about twelve hours of even ebb and flow, six hours each on the average and taking the world as a whole: because the earth takes twenty-four hours to go round.

But if you were to act upon that first principle *only* in any one part of the world, and to say without testing the thing in practice, "I can calculate the tide theoretically," you would very often wreck your ship. For many other principles come into play in the matter of the tide besides this twelve-hour period. In one case the tide will be delayed by shoals or by the current of a river. In another there may be two or three tides meeting. In a third the sea will be so locked that there will be hardly any tide for many hours, and then a rush at the end – and so on.

Now it is just the same with Economics. Your economic first principle makes you come to such and such a *theoretical* conclusion. But there are a lot of other first principles at work, and they may modify the effect *in practice* to any extent. When people object to "theoretical dreaming," as they call it, they mean the bad habit of thinking that one conclusion from one particular set of first principles is sufficient and will apply to any set of circumstances. It never does. One has always to watch the thing in practice, and see what other forces come in.

In the political applications of Economic Science we have to deal with the effect of human society upon Economic Law. For instance: Economic Law tells us that, given a certain standard of living for labour – the "worth while" of labour – and a certain minimum profit without which capital will not accumulate – the "worth while" of capital – there is, as we have seen, a lowest limit of production; a set of conditions below which production will not take place. Land which is below a certain standard of fertility will not be farmed; a vein of metal below a certain standard of yield will not be mined under such and such social conditions. But all circumstances in which production has greater advantages than this lowest limit produce a surplus value called "Rent." That is an economic law, and it is always true.

But it does not follow that the owner of the land, for instance, will get the full economic rent of the land. There may be customs in society, or laws, by which he is compelled to share with the tenant. The theoretical economic rent is there all right, but one cannot deduce from this truth that the landlord will necessarily and always get the whole of it. And so it is with every other political application.

Having said so much by way of Preface, let us turn to the particular problems, and first of all consider the idea which underlies all practical economic conclusions, the idea of PROPERTY.

The very first governing condition of economic production and distribution in the real world is the condition of *control*. Who *controls* the process of production in any particular Society? Who in it owns (that is, has the right and power to use or leave idle, to distribute or withhold) the means of production, the stores of food and clothing, and houses and machinery? On the answer to that question depends the economic structure of a society. This control is called "Property," and as the first thing we have to study in practical Economics is the character of Property, we will make that the first division of our political applications.

I

PROPERTY:
THE CONTROL OF WEALTH

A LL the political application of Economics – that is, all the appli-cation of Economic Science to the conduct of families in the State – turns on The Control of Wealth, and of the things necessary to make wealth.

The first thing to grasp is that *someone* must control every piece of wealth if it is to be used to any purpose. Every bundle of economic values in the community must be under the control of some human will; otherwise those pieces of wealth "run to waste," that is, are consumed without use to mankind. For instance, a ton of threshed wheat represents a bundle of economic values. It represents a piece of wealth equivalent, in currency measure, to say £16. If no one has the right to decide upon its preservation and use, when and how it is to be kept dry and free from vermin, when and how it is to be ground and the flour made into bread, then it will rot or be eaten by rats, and in a short time its economic values will have disappeared. It will be worthless. The £16 worth of wealth will have been "consumed without use"; in plain language, wasted. But if wealth were all wasted humanity would die out. So men must, of necessity, arrange for a *control* of all wealth, and this they do by laws which fix the control of one parcel of wealth by one authority, of another by another; men make laws allowing such control by some people and preventing attempted control by other people not authorised. This lawful control over a piece of wealth we call "Property" in it.

Thus, the coal in your cellar which you have bought is by our laws your property. It is for you to burn it as you want it and when you choose. If another person comes in and takes some of it without your leave, to burn it as *he* chooses, he is called a thief and punished as such. The coal in the Admiralty Stores is State property. The State has the right to decide into what ships it is to be put and how and when it is to be burnt, and so on. But whether the control is in private hands such as yours, or in the naval authorities who are officers of the State, control there must always be.

When people say that they want to "abolish property," or that "There ought to be no property," they mean *Private* property: the right of individuals, or families, or corporations to control wealth. Property in the full sense, meaning the control of wealth by *someone*, whether the State, or private individuals, or what not, is inevitable, and is necessary in every human society. So, granting that property must exist, we will first examine the various forms it may take.

At the beginning of our examination we noticed that wealth, owned and controlled by whoever it may be – the State, or an individual, or a corporation – is of two kinds. There is the wealth which will be consumed in enjoyment and the wealth which will be consumed in producing future wealth.

The wealth which will be consumed in producing future wealth is, as we have seen, called "Capital." For instance: if a man has a ton of wheat and eats half of it while he is doing nothing but taking a holiday, or doing work which has some moral but no material effect – that is not Capital. But if he uses the other half to keep himself alive while he is ploughing and sowing for a future harvest, and keeps a little of it for the seed of that harvest, all that he so uses is *Capital*. Since control of wealth is necessary, no matter of what kind the wealth be, it is clear that there must be property not only in what is about to be consumed in enjoyment but also in Capital. Someone, then, must own Capital.

But here comes in a very important addition. The fertility of land, space upon which to build, mines of metal, water power, natural opportunities of any kind and natural forces, *though they are not wealth*,† are the necessary conditions for producing wealth. Someone, therefore, must control these also: someone must have the power of

---

† It is important to keep our ideas rigidly clear on this point. You can exchange a piece of fertile land for some set of values. Yet it is not *wealth*. It is not matter transposed from a condition where it is less useful to a condition where it is more useful to man. See the definitions in the first chapter, "What is wealth?"

saying, "This field shall be ploughed and sown thus and thus. This waterfall must be made to turn this turbine in such and such a spot, and the power developed must be applied thus and thus." For if no one had such power the fertility of the land, the force of the stream, would be wasted.

Property, therefore, extends over two fields, one of which is itself divided into two parts. A.—It extends over natural forces. B.—It extends over wealth, and, in the case of B, wealth, it extends over B.1, wealth to be used for future production (which kind of wealth, when it is so used, is called "Capital"), and also B.2, wealth which is going to be consumed without the attempt to produce anything else: consumed, as the phrase goes, "in enjoyment."† Natural forces may be grouped, as we have grouped them in the first part of this book, under the conventional term "Land." So Property covers Land and Capital, as well as Wealth to be consumed without the attempt to produce other wealth. You may put the whole thing in a diagram thus:—

PROPERTY

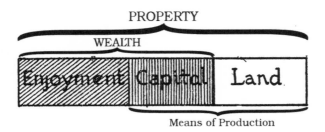

Means of Production

In studying the social effects of Property it is convenient to group together Land and that part of wealth which is used for further production and is called Capital, and to call the two "the means of production": because, in a great many social problems the important point is not who owns the Capital separately or the Land separately, but who owns the whole bundle of things which constitute the Means of Production, without which no production can take place.

---

† "Enjoyment" does not mean, in this connection, pleasure, happiness. It is a conventional phrase to mean "consumption *not* directed to the making of further wealth." Thus the wealth consumed at a boring dinner party is consumed in "enjoyment."

For instance: supposing a man owns a hundred acres of fertile land, that is his property, and though we call it wealth in ordinary conversation it is not real wealth at all. It is only the opportunity for producing wealth. If no one worked on that land, if no one even worked so little as to take the trouble of picking fruit off the trees or cutting the grass or looking after animals on it, it would be worth nothing. Supposing another man to own the stores of food and the houses and the clothing necessary for the livelihood of the labourers on the land, and also the horses and the ploughs and the stores of seeds necessary for farming, then that man owns the Capital only. But to the *labourers* the important thing is that someone else owns the Means of Production, *without which they cannot live,* and they are equally dependent whether one or many control or own the Means of Production in any particular case. *Their* condition has for its main character *the fact that they do not own the "Means of Production."*

Labour must be kept going. That is, human energy, for producing wealth from land, while it is at work, waiting between one harvest and another, will consume part of the stores of food and some proportion of the housing (which is a perishable thing, though it only perishes slowly) and of the clothing, and of the seed, etc. So we have to examine the various ways in which labour (which is not wealth) and land (which is not wealth) and capital (which *is* wealth) may be controlled.

There are three main types of human society which differ according to the way in which control is exercised over these three factors of Labour, Capital and Land. These three types are:—

1. THE SERVILE STATE: that is, the state in which the material Means of Production are the property of men who also own the human agents of Production.

2. THE CAPITALIST STATE: that is, the state in which the material Means of Production are the property of a few, and the numerous human agents of Production are free, but without property.

3. THE DISTRIBUTIVE STATE: that is, the state in which the material means of Production are owned by the free human agents of Production.

There is also a fourth imaginary kind of state which has never come into being, called the SOCIALIST or COMMUNIST STATE. We will examine this in its right place, but the only three *actual* states of which we know anything in history and can deal with as real human experiences, are these three just described: the *Servile* State, the *Capitalist* State, and the *Distributive* State.

But, before going farther, we must get hold of a very important principle, which is this:—

THE NATURE OF AN ECONOMIC SOCIETY IS NOT DETERMINED BY ITS ARRANGEMENTS BEING UNIVERSAL, THAT IS, APPLYING WITHOUT EXCEPTION TO ALL THE FAMILIES OF THE STATE, BUT ONLY BY THEIR APPLYING TO WHAT IS CALLED THE DETERMINING NUMBER OF THE FAMILIES OF THE STATE: THAT IS, IN SO GREAT A PROPORTION AS TO COLOUR AND GIVE ITS FORM TO THE WHOLE SOCIETY.

No one can exactly define the amount of this "determining number," but we all know in practice what it means. For instance: we say the English are a tall race, from 5½ feet to 6 feet high. But that does not mean necessarily that the majority of the people are over 5½ feet. You have, of course, to exclude the children, and there are a great number of very short people and a few very tall people. It means that the general impression conveyed when you mix with English people – the size of the doors and the implements with which men work, and the clothes that are produced, and the rest of it – turn upon the general experience that you are dealing with a race of about that size – 5½ to 6 feet. Or again, you say that the *determining* number or proportion of our society speaks English. That does not mean that they all speak English. Some are dumb; some speak Welsh or Gaelic. Many speak with such an accent that others with a different accent find it difficult to understand them. Yet it is true to say that the society in which we live speaks English.

Now it is exactly the same with the economic conditions of society. You may have a society in which there is a certain number of slaves, and yet it is not a slave-owning society, because the number of free men is so great as to give a general tone of freedom. Or you have, as we have in England, a great deal of property owned by the State – barracks and battleships and arsenals, some of the forests, and so on – but we do not say that England is economically a State-owned society, because the *determining* proportion of property is not owned by the State but by private people. The general effect produced is one of private ownership and not of State ownership.

One more principle must be set down before we go farther, and that is that almost any society is mixed. A society of which the determining proportion is slave-owning will yet certainly have a proportion of free men; for if it did not there would be no one to own the slaves. In the same way what is called a Capitalist Society, which I will describe in a moment (and which is the society in which we now live in England) has a great number of people not living under purely capitalist conditions. It is mixed.

But, though only a *determining number* is required to mark the character of a particular society, and though every society is *mixed* in its character, it remains true that all societies we know of, in the past or the present, fall into one of these three groups – the Servile (that is, slave-owning), the Capitalist, and the Distributive.

The definition of these three systems is as follows:—

1. In the Slave-owning Society, or Servile State, a certain minority owns a determining amount of the wealth and also of land – that is, the means of production (land and capital) and the wealth ready for consumption in enjoyment. The rest of the community is compelled by positive law to give its labour for the advantage of these few owners; and this rest of the community are, by economic definition (whether they call themselves by the actual name or not), slaves: that is, they can be compelled to work for the owners, and can be punished by law if they do not work for the owners.

2. In the Capitalist State a determining number of the families or individuals are free; that is, they cannot be compelled by positive law to work for anybody. They are at liberty to make a contract. Each can say to an owner of land or capital: "I will work for you for so much reward, such and such a proportion of the wealth I produce. If you will not give me that I will not work at all," and no one can punish him for the refusal.

But the mark of the Capitalist State is that a determining amount of land and capital is owned by a small number of people, and that the rest of the people – much the greater number – though free, cannot get food or housing or clothing except in so far as the owners of these things (that is, of the means of production) choose to give it them. In such a state of society the people who own nothing, or next to nothing, are free to make a contract and to say: "I will work on your farm" (for instance) "if you will give me half or three-quarters of the harvest. If you will not, I will not work for you." But this contract is bound by a very hard condition, for if they push their refusal to the limit and continue not to work they will starve, and they will not be able to get housing against the weather or clothes to wear.

We are living today, in England especially, in such a Capitalist State. In such a state the free men who contract to sell their labour often have a certain very small proportion of things on which they can live for a short time. They have a suit of clothes and perhaps a little money with which they can purchase a few days' livelihood – some of them more, some of them less. But the tone or colour of the society is given by the fact that *the great majority, though free, are dispossessed of the means of production, and therefore of livelihood, and that a small minority controls these things.*

The word "Capitalism" does not mean that there exists capital in such a society. Capital exists in all societies. It is a necessary part of human society and of the production of wealth, without which no society can live at all. The word "Capitalism" is only "shorthand" for the condition we have just described: a condition where capital and land are in few hands though all men are free.

3. The Distributive State is a state in which a determining number of the citizens, a number sufficient to colour the habits, laws and conditions of the whole society, is possessed of the means of production, as private property, divided among the various families. The word "distributive" is an ugly, long word, only used for want of a better; but the reason that we have to use such a tiresome word is an odd and paradoxical reason well worth grasping. The Distributive State is the natural state of mankind. Men are happiest in such conditions; they can fulfil their being best and are most perfectly themselves when they are owners and free. Now whenever you have natural and good conditions, not only in Economics but in any other aspect of life, it is very difficult to find a word for it. There is always a word ready for odd, unnatural conditions: but it is often difficult

to find a word for conditions normal to our human nature. For instance: we have the words "dwarf" and "giant," but we have no similar common, short word to describe people of ordinary stature. So it is with the Distributive State. We have to use an ugly new word, because men more or less take for granted this state of affairs in their minds, and have never thought out a special word for it.

However, a name it must have; so let us agree to call that kind of society in which most men are *really* free and dignified and full citizens, not only possessing rights before the law, but *owning*, so that they are at no other man's orders but can live independently, "The Distributive State."

Then we have these three main types of Society within human experience: the Servile, the Capitalist, the Distributive.

To put these three estates clearly before our minds, let us describe the kind of thing you would see in any one of the three.

In the Servile State, as you travelled through the country, you would most ordinarily see working on the fields men who were the slaves of a master. That master would own the land and the seed, and the food and the houses, and the horses and ploughs and everything, and these men you would see working would be compelled to work for their master, and he would have the right by law to punish them if they did not.

If you were in a Capitalist State (as we are in England) the men you would see working would, as a rule, be earning what are called "wages," that is, an allowance (actually of money but immediately translated into food and clothes and house-room and the rest), which allowance would be paid to them at fairly short intervals, and without which they could not live. The ploughs and horses with which they would be working, the seed they would be sowing, the houses they lived in would be the property of another man owning this *capital*, and therefore called "The Capitalist." If you asked any one of these men who were working whether he were *compelled* to work by law he would indignantly tell you that he was not. For he is a free man; his wages are paid him as a result of a contract; he has said: "I will work for you for so much," and no one could compel him to work if he did not choose to work. But in this state of society a man without capital must make a contract of this sort in order to live at all. He is not compelled by law to work for another, but he is compelled by the necessity of living to work for another.

Lastly, if you were travelling through a Distributive State (Denmark is the best example of such a state in modern Europe) you would find that the man working on the land was himself the owner of the land, and also of the seed and of the horses and the houses, and all the rest of it. He would be a free man working for his own advantage and for nobody else's. He would also have a share in the factories of the country and be a part owner in the local dairies, sharing the profit of those dairies where the milk of many farms is gathered together, turned into butter and cheese, and sold.

This is what we mean by the three types of State. In each you would find many exceptions, but each has its *determining number* – of slaves in the one case, wage earners in the other, and independent men in the third.

We will now take each of these three kinds of State separately and see the good and evil of them and what the consequences of them are.

II

THE SERVILE STATE

THE Servile State is that which was found among our forefathers everywhere. It is the Servile State in which we Europeans all lived when we were pagan two thousand years ago. For instance: In old pagan Italy before it became Christian, or in old pagan Greece – both of them the best countries in the world of their time and both of them, as you know, the origins of our own civilisation – most of the people you would have seen working at anything were slaves, and above the slaves were the owners: the free men.

Since we are talking of the political applications of political economy, we have to consider *human happiness,* which is the object of all human living; and when we talk of "advantage" or "disadvantage" in any particular economic state we mean its greater or less effect on human happiness.

The great disadvantage of the slave-owning state is clearly apparent: in it the mass of men are degraded: they are not citizens: they cannot exercise their own wills. This is so evident and great an evil that it must be set against all the advantages we are about to notice. Slavery is a most unhappy condition in so far as it wounds human honour and offends human dignity; and that is why the Christian religion gradually dissolved slavery in the process of many centuries: slavery is not sufficiently consistent with the idea of man's being made in the image of God. Slavery can also be materially unhappy, if the masters are cruel or negligent. The great mass of slaves in such a society might be, at the caprice of their masters, very unhappy; and under bad phases of those societies they *were* very unhappy.

But we must not be misled by the ideas that have grown up around the word "slave" in the modern mind. Because we have no one in England today who is called a slave and bought or sold as a slave, and no one is yet compelled by law to work for another man, therefore we regard slavery as something odd and alien; and because it is natural to dislike things which are odd and alien, unaccustomed, we think of slavery as something simply bad.

That is a great mistake. The Servile State had – and, if it comes back, will have again – two great advantages: which were *personal security* and *general stability*.

"Personal security" means a condition in which everybody, master and man, is free from grave anxiety upon the future: can expect regular food and lodging and a continuance of his regular way of life.

"General stability" means the continuance of all society in one fashion, without the violent ups and downs of competition and without the friction of unwilling constantly interrupted labour – as in strikes and lock-outs.

In the Servile State work always got done and was done regularly. The owners knew "where they were." With so much land and so many slaves they were sure of a certain average annual produce. On the whole it was to the advantage of a man to keep his slaves alive and fairly well fed and housed. Also, the human relation came in, and a man and his slave, in the better and simpler forms of the Servile State, would often be friends and were usually in the same relation as people are today with their dependants. For instance: in well-to-do houses of the Servile State we know from history that certain slaves were often the tutors of the children, and thus had a very important and respectable position, and there were other slaves who acted as good musicians and architects and artists. There was always the feeling of a fixed social difference between slave and free, but this did not necessarily nor perhaps usually lead to great unhappiness.

This stability and security which slave-owning gave to all society (to the owned to some extent, and to the owners altogether) also produced a very valuable effect, which is, the presence of *leisure*. Because revenue was fairly certain, because this kind of arrangement prevented violent fluctuation of fortune, competition in excess, and the rest of it, therefore was there a considerable proportion of people at any time who had ample opportunity for study, for cultivating good tastes, for writing and building well, and judging well, and

– what is very important – for conducting the affairs of the State without haste or the panic and folly of haste.

One alleged *economic* disadvantage of slave-owning must be looked at narrowly before we leave this description of the Servile State.

One often hears it said that slave labour is less productive than free labour, that is, labour working at a wage under Capitalism. People sometimes point to modern examples of this contrast, saying that places like the Southern States of America, where slave labour was used a lifetime ago, were less productive than the Northern States, where labour was free. But though this is true of particular moments in history, it is not generally true. Free labour working at a wage under the first institution of Capitalism – when, for instance, a body of capitalists are beginning to develop a new country with hired free men to work for them – will be full of energy and highly productive. But when what is called "free labour" – that is, men without property working by contract for a wage – gets into routine and habit, it is doubtful whether it is more productive than slave labour. It is accompanied by a great deal of ill-will. There is perpetual interruption by strikes, and lock-outs,† and the process of production cannot be as minutely and absolutely directed by the small and leisured class as can slave labour. *There is no reason why a free man working for another's profit should do his best.* On the contrary, he has every reason to work as little as possible, while a slave can be compelled to work hard.

But whether slave labour be more or less productive is not so important as the two points mentioned above, of advantage and disadvantage. The *disadvantages,* as we have seen, are (1) that it offends our human love of honour and independence, degrading the mass of men, and (2) that it is so terribly liable to abuse in the hands of cruel or stupid owners, or in conditions where great gangs of

---

† A "Strike" is a modern English word (only used where the English language is spoken), and signifying the refusal of the free labourers to sell their labour for the amount hitherto given. They cease work, thereby interrupting the profits of the capitalist who furnishes them with food, clothing, etc., in the shape of wages. They do so in the hope of compelling him, by loss of profits during their idleness, to pay them more.

A "Lock-out" is a modern English word now used all over the world to signify an action of the capitalist refusing to pay his workmen what they have hitherto received,

slaves grow up under one owner who can know nothing about them personally and is therefore indifferent to their fate. The *advantages* are security and stability, running as a note throughout society and showing themselves especially in the leisure of the owning classes, with all the good fruits of leisure in taste, literary and artistic. It was a society based on slavery which produced what is perhaps the best fruit of leisure, and that is the profound and fruitful thinking out of the great human problems. All the great philosophy and art of the ancients was worked out by the free owners in the slave-owning states, and so was the best literature ever made.

Trévoux, Rue du Port.

---

and hoping to starve them into accepting lower wages by "locking them out" of his factory until they submit.

Strikes are only possible when the labourers have accumulated some capital on which to live during the struggle. This they accumulate by contributions to the common fund of a Trades Union while still in employment. A Lock-out is only possible from the fact that such funds are small and soon exhausted.

III

THE CAPITALIST STATE

THE Capitalist State is that one in which though all men are free (that is, though no one is compelled to work for another by law, nor anyone compelled to support another), yet a few owners of the land and capital have working for them the great mass of the people who own little or nothing and receive a *wage* to keep them alive: that is, a part only of the wealth they produce, the rest going as rent and profit to the owners.

The Capitalist State is a recent phenomenon compared with the great length of known recorded history. It is a modern phenomenon produced by our white race alone, by no means covering the whole of that race, nor the most of it, but of great interest to us in England because we alone are, of all nations, an almost purely capitalist society.

Here again we can tabulate the advantages and disadvantages.

The chief moral advantage of Capitalism as compared with the Slave-owning State is that *every man, however poor, feels himself to be free and to that extent saves his honour.* He may be compelled by poverty to suffer a very hard bargain; he may see himself producing wealth for other men, of which wealth he is only allowed to keep a portion for himself. To that extent he is "exploited," as the phrase goes. He feels himself the victim of a certain injustice. He remains poor in spite of all his labour, and the man for whom he works grows rich. But, after all, it is a contract which the free workman has made, and he has made it as a citizen. If those who own nothing, or next to nothing, in a capitalist state (this great majority is technically called in economic language "the *proletariat*") organise, they can bargain, as our great Trade Unions do, with the few owners of their means of livelihood and of production, and be fairly certain, for some little time ahead, of a reasonable livelihood.

Another advantage of Capitalism, purely economic, is the *effectiveness of human energy* under this system, at least, *in the first part of its development*. We spoke of this in the last section.

But the disadvantages are very grave indeed.

Under Capitalism the capitalist himself acts competitively and for a profit. He does not, like the slave-owner, direct a regular, simple machine which works evenly year in and year out. He is perpetually struggling to rise; or suffering, through the rise of others, a fall of fortune. He is always on the look-out to buy labour as cheaply as he can and then to sell the product as dearly as he can. There is thus a perpetual gamble going on, the owners of Capital rapidly growing rich and poor by turns and a general insecurity gradually poisoning all the owning part of society. A far worse insecurity affects the propertyless majority. The Proletariat – that is, the mass of the State – lives perpetually under the fear of falling into unemployment and starvation. The lash urging the workman to his fullest effort is this dread of misery. At first that lash urges men to intense effort, but later it destroys their energy. Capitalism was marked by nothing more striking when it first arose than by the immense expansion of wealth and population which followed it. In every district which fell under the capitalist system this expansion of total wealth and of total population could be observed; and England, which has become completely capitalist, had in the hey-day of its Capitalism – up to the present generation – a more rapid rate of expansion in wealth and population than any other ancient people. But already the tide has turned, and the inhumanity of such a life is beginning to breed everywhere an ill-ease and revolt which threaten our civilisation.

The disadvantages of Capitalism are, in the long run, so great that now, after not more than a lifetime of complete Capitalism, and that in only one State – the English State – nearly everybody is profoundly discontented with it and many people are in violent rebellion against it. This grinding and increasing insecurity which attaches to the Capitalist System is killing it. No one is safe for the morrow. Perpetual competition, increasing with every increase of energy, has led to a chaos in human society such as there never was before. The mass of the people, not being slaves, cannot be certain that they will be kept alive. They live in a state of perpetual anxiety as to whether their employment will continue; while among the owners themselves the same anxiety exists in another form. The competition among them gets more and more severe. The number of owners gets less, and even the richest of them is more insecure than were the moderately rich of a generation ago. All society is like a boiling pot, with individuals suddenly coming into great wealth from below and then dropping out again; the whole State suffers from an increasing absence of leisure and an increasing turmoil.

There is, then, this very grave disadvantage of insecurity everywhere, and particularly for the mass of the people, who live under permanent conditions of insecurity; nearly all the wage-earners have had experience at some time, longer or shorter, of insufficiency through unemployment. Capitalism leaves free men under a sense of acute grievance (which they would *not* feel if they were slaves, accustomed to a regular and fixed status in society), and, what is worse, Capitalism *in its later stages* need not provide for the livelihood of the mass of citizens, and, in effect, *does not* so provide.

The magnitude of these evils is obvious. A man who is a free man, a citizen, able in theory to take part in the life of the State, equal with the richest man before the law, yet finds himself living on a precarious amount of necessaries of life doled out as wages week after week; he sees his labour exploited by others and suffers from a sense of injustice and oppression. The wealth of the small, owning, class does not seem a natural adjunct to its social position, as it does in the slave-owning state; for there is no tradition behind that class; it has no "status," that is, no general respect paid to it as something naturally – or, at any rate, traditionally – superior to the rest of men. Many a modern millionaire capitalist, exploiting the labour of thousands of his fellows, is of a lower culture than most of his labourers; and, what is more, he may in a few years have lost all his economic position and have been succeeded by another, even baser than himself. How can the masses feel respect for such a man in such a position of chance advantage?

It is inevitable that a moral evil of this sort should make the whole State unstable. You cannot make of great differences in wealth between citizens a stable state of affairs, save by breeding respect for the owners of great wealth. But the more the turmoil of Capitalism increases the less respect these owners of great wealth either deserve or obtain: the less do they form a class, and the less do they preserve traditions of any kind. And yet it is under these very conditions of Capitalism that there is a greater disparity of wealth than ever the world knew before! It is clear that society in such a condition must be as unstable as an explosive.

So much for the first great disadvantage of Capitalism, chaos. But the second main disadvantage – the fact that Capitalism in its later stages ceases to guarantee the livelihood of the people – is a little less easy to understand. Indeed, most people who discuss Capitalism, even when they strongly oppose it, seem unable to grasp this second disadvantage – so let us examine it closely.

I have said that Capitalism, in its later stages, *does not provide for the maintenance of the mass of the people.*

To see how true this is, consider an extreme case.

Supposing one man were to own all the means of production, and supposing he were to have in his possession one machine which could produce in an indefinite amount all that human beings need in order to live. Then there would be no economic reason why this one man should provide wealth for anyone except himself and his family. He might turn out enough things to support a few others whom he wanted for private servants or to amuse him, but there would be no reason why he should support the masses around him.

Now it is true that we have not yet come, under Capitalism, to so extreme a case. But the moral applies, though modified, to Capitalism in its last stages, when very few men control the means of production, when machinery has become very efficient, and when the great mass of people are dependent upon employment by the capitalist for their existence.

Consider that it is of the essence of Capitalism to keep wages down, that is, to buy labour cheap. Therefore, the labourer who actually produces, say, boots cannot afford to buy a sufficient amount of the boots which he himself has made. The capitalist controlling the boot-making machinery, when he has provided himself with a dozen pair of boots, and the working classes of the community with such boots as their wages permit them to buy, must either try to sell the extra boots abroad (and that outlet can't last long) or stop making them. He has restricted the home market by the necessity of cheap labour, and you have the absurd position of men making more goods than they need, and yet having less of those goods available for themselves than they need: the labourer producing, or able to produce, every year enough clothing for ten years, and yet not being able to afford sufficient for one: the labourer producing or able to produce ten good overcoats, yet not able to buy one.

So under Capitalism in its last stages you have the abnormal position of millions of men ready to make the necessaries of life, of machinery ready to produce those necessaries, of raw material standing ready to be worked up by the machinery if only labourers could be put on, and yet all the machinery standing idle, the wealth not being produced, and the mass who could produce it going hungry and ill-shod and badly clothed. And the more Capitalism develops the more that state of things will develop with it.

Now this gradual lessening of purchasing power on the part of the working masses under Capitalism is *the destruction of the home market*. Low wages make great masses of English bootmakers unable to buy all the boots they would. Therefore the capitalist who owns the boot-making machinery must try to sell his surplus abroad. But the foreign countries, as they grow capitalist, suffer from the same trouble: property being badly distributed and the wage-earners kept as low as possible, their power to buy foreign goods also diminishes. Thus you have *gradual destruction of the foreign market*. You get in the long run the full working of what we will call the *"Capitalist Paradox,"* which is that Capitalism is a way of producing wealth which, in the long run, prevents people from obtaining the wealth produced and prevents the owner of the wealth from finding a market.

There is no doubt that, on the balance, the disadvantages of Capitalism have proved, even after its short trial, overwhelmingly greater than the advantages.

Capitalism arose in small beginnings rather more than 250 years ago. It grew strong and covered the greater part of the community (in England, at least) about 100 years ago. It came to its highest development in our own time; and it is already doomed. People cannot bear it any longer. Future historians looking back upon our time will be astonished at the immense productivity of Capitalism, the enormous addition to wealth which it made, and to population, in its early phases; but perhaps they will be still more astonished at the pace at which it ran down at its end. Urged by the extreme human suffering, moral and material, which Capitalism now produces, remedies have been proposed, the chief of which is generally called Socialism, or, in its fully developed form, Communism.

But before we talk of this supposed remedy, which has never been put into practice (it is an imaginary state of things) we must describe the third form of state – the Distributive State.

KERSEY

IV

THE DISTRIBUTIVE STATE

A state of society in which the families composing it are, in a
determining number, owners of the land and the means of production as well as themselves the human agents of production (that
is, the people who by their human energy produce wealth with those
means of production), is probably the oldest, and certainly the most
commonly found of all states of society. It is a state of society which
you get all through the East, all through Asia, and all the primitive
states we know. It is the state to which men try to return, as a rule,
after they have blundered into any other, though the first state we
described – the Servile State – runs it very close as a thing suitable
to human nature; for we know that the Servile State did also last for
centuries quite normally and stably in the Pagan past.

The reason men commonly adopt the Distributive form of
society, and tend to return to it if they can, is that the advantages it
presents seem greater in most men's eyes than its disadvantages.

The advantages are these:—

It gives freedom: that is, the exercise of one's will. A family
possessed of the means of production – the simplest form of which is
the possession of land and of the implements and capital for working
the land – cannot be controlled by others. Of course, various producers specialise, and through exchange one with the other they become
more or less interdependent, but still, each one can live "on his own":
each one can stand out, if necessary, from pressure exercised against
him by another. He can say: "If you will not take my surplus as
against your surplus I shall be the poorer; but at least I can live."

Societies of this kind are not only free, but also, what goes with
freedom, elastic – that is, they mould themselves easily to changed
conditions. The individual, or the family, controlling his or its own
means of production, can choose what he will do best, and can exercise
his faculties, if he has sufficient knowledge, to the best advantage.

This arrangement also gives security, though not as much security as the Servile State. Men in this position of ownership are not in dread of the immediate future. They can carry on. They may, if they choose, make a reserve of their produce to carry them over moments of difficulty. For instance, they will probably have each a reserve of food to carry them over a bad harvest or some natural disaster. Further, it is found in practice that societies of this kind continue for centuries without much change. They go on for generations with a property well divided among them and everybody free, so far as economic situation is concerned. No such society has ever been destroyed except by some great shock; and so long as every shock can be warded off, this system of having the land and the means of production controlled by the mass of the citizens as private owners is enduring. There are districts of Europe today where the system has continued from beyond the memory of man. Such a little state as Andorra is an example, and many of the Swiss valleys. Further, when the system has been laboriously reconstructed, when the mass of families who used to be dispossessed have been again put into possession of land and the means of production, we find that the state arrived at is stable.

The best example of that sort of reconstruction today is to be found in Denmark, but you have it also in a less marked fashion in most parts of France and in most of the Valley of the Rhine, in Belgium and Holland, in Norway, and in many other places. Wherever it has been settled it has taken root firmly.

The disadvantages of such a system are, first, that though in practice it is found usually stable, yet in theory it is not necessarily stable, and in practice also there are some communities the social character of which is such that the system cannot be established permanently.

It is obvious that, with land and the means of production well distributed among the various families, a few may by luck or special perseverance and cunning, tend to buy up the land and implements of their less fortunate neighbours, and nothing will prevent this but a set of laws backed up by strong public opinion. In other words, people must desire this state of society, and desire it strongly in order to maintain it; and if the desire for ownership and freedom is weak this distributive arrangement will not last.

In the absence of special laws, and a public opinion to back them, the idler or the least competent or least lucky of the owners will gradually lose their ownership to the more industrious or the more cunning or more fortunate.

Another disadvantage which has often been pointed out is that a state of society of this sort, though usually stable and enduring, falls into a routine (that is, into a traditional way of doing things), which it is very difficult to change. The small owner will not have the same opportunities for travel and for wide experience as the rich man has, and he will tend to go on as his fathers did, and therefore when some new invention arises outside his society he will be slow to adopt it. In this way his society becomes less able to defend itself from predatory neighbours and goes under in war. For a society of this kind is unfitted to the discovery of new things. Contented men feel no special spur to discover or to act on such discovery. That is why we find societies in which land and all the other means of production are well distributed among the greater part of the families of the State becoming too con-servative – that is, unwilling to change even for their own advantage.

This, of course, is not universally true. For instance: no society in Europe has made more progress in agriculture than the Danish society of small owners. But, take the world all over, this kind of state is usually backward, that is, slow to take up improvements in produc-tion and to avail itself of new discoveries in physical science.

There is also another disadvantage which the Distributive State has when it is in competition with a Capitalist State, or even a Servile State, and that is *the difficulty of getting a very large number of small owners to put their money together for any great purpose.* The small owner will probably have less opportunities for instruction and judgment than the few directing rich men of a Capitalist or Servile State, and even if he is, on the average, as well educated as these rich men in neighbouring states, it will be more difficult to get a great number of small owners to act together than to persuade a few large owners to act together. Therefore highly capitalist States, such as England, will be found more enterprising than less capitalist States in their invest-ments and commerce. They will open up new countries more rapidly, and will get possession of the best markets.

Lastly, this disadvantage attaches to the Distributive State – that it is not so easy in it to collect great funds for war or for national defence, or for any other purpose, as it is in a Capitalist or Servile State. You cannot tax a Distributive State as highly as you can tax a Capitalist State. The reason is obvious enough. A family with, say, £400 a year finds it terribly difficult – almost impossible – to pay out £100 a year in taxation. They live on a certain modest scale to which all their lives are fitted, and which does not leave very much margin for taxation. If you have a million such families with a total income of £400 millions you may collect from them, say, a tenth of their wealth in a year – £40 millions – but you will hardly be able to collect a quarter – £100 millions.

But another society with exactly the same amount of total wealth, £400 millions a year, only divided into very rich and very poor, a society in which there are, say, 1,000 very rich families with £300,000 a year each, and a million families with rather less than £100 a year each, is in quite a different situation. You need not tax at all the million people with a hundred a year each, but the rich people, who between them have £300,000,000 a year, can easily be taxed a quarter of their whole wealth; for a rich man always has a much larger margin, the loss of which he does not really feel.

By a very curious paradox, which it would take much too long to go into in detail, but which it is amusing to notice, this power of taxing a very highly capitalist community is one of the things which is beginning to handicap our capitalist societies today against the Distributive societies. It used to be all the other way, and it seemed common sense that countries where you could levy large sums for State purposes of war or peace would win against countries where you could not levy such sums for public purposes. But the fact that you can tax so very highly a society of a few rich and many poor has been shown in the last few years to have most unexpected results. The very rich men pay all right; but the drain on the total resources of the wealth of the State weakens it.

The money raised by taxation is spent on State servants – many of them inefficient and idle.

Since it is so easy to raise large sums, there is a temptation to indulge in all sorts of expensive State schemes, many of which come to nothing. And this power of easy taxation, which was a strength, becomes a weakness.

No one suspected this until taxation rose to its present height, but now it is clearly apparent; and we in England might perhaps be in a better way later on if there had been as much resistance to high taxation here as there has been in countries where property is better distributed.

V

SOCIALISM

IT remains to deal with a certain remedy which some people have imagined would get rid of all the disadvantages of Capitalism once and for all. This remedy is called "Socialism," and Socialism, as we shall see in a moment, must mean ultimately *Communism.*

No one has ever succeeded in putting this remedy for the evils of Capitalism into practice, and (though the matter is still very much disputed) it looks more and more as though no one would ever be able to put it into practice.

We have seen what the evils of Capitalism were and how they have exasperated nearly everyone who has become subject to a capitalist state of society. There is the increasing insecurity which everybody feels – all the proletariat and many of the capitalists as well – whilst there is the necessary tendency of Capitalism to leave a larger and larger proportion of people unproductive, not making the wealth which is necessary for their support, and therefore either kept in idleness by Doles out of the wealth which is still produced (a process which cannot go on for ever) or starving. Pretty well everyone wants to get rid of these evils and to get out of the Capitalist System, and this idea of Socialism which we are going to examine seemed, when it was first put forward, an easy and obvious shortcut out of the Capitalist muddle. When we have looked into it, we shall see how and why Socialism does not, in practice, turn out to be a shortcut at all, but a blind alley.

***

Ever since men began to live in societies and to leave records, you will find the poorer people, when their poverty became intolerable, clamouring for a division of the wealth which the more fortunate enjoy.

That is the main, obvious remedy to inequality of wealth; to divide it up again. But such a scheme has nothing to do with Socialism, and must not be mistaken for Socialism.

The Socialist theory was invented, or at any rate was first put clearly, by a man of genius, Louis Blanc, who was Scotch on his father's side and French on his mother's. He lived rather less than a hundred years ago and the scheme which he and those around him started was this:—

The Officers of the State were to own all the Means of Production – machinery and land and stores of food, etc. – and they alone should be allowed to own it. Individuals and families and corporations might consume that portion of produced wealth allotted them by the State after it had been produced, *but they might not use it for making future wealth. Any wealth used for the making of future wealth, that is, Capital in any form, was to be handed over to the officers of the State; and all land and natural forces were to be owned forever by the State.* That scheme is SOCIALISM, and from that principle all Socialist ideas flow.

In this way, it was claimed, there would be no division of society into Capitalists and Proletarians, no chaos of competition with its alternating riches and ruin; insecurity would be done away with, and insufficiency as well. Everyone in the country would be a worker, the State itself would be the Universal Capitalist. So there would be no struggle of capitalists going up and down one against the other, and no unemployment or lack of necessaries for anyone.

Among the energetic and keen set of men who surrounded Blanc in Paris was a certain Mordecai, who wrote under the name his father had assumed, that of "Marx." He wrote (in German) a very long and detailed book describing the whole scheme, as well as describing the evils of Capitalism, and showing how this scheme would remedy those evils. His book was pushed forward by the people who were converted to the idea, and that is why the theory of Socialism is now often called "Marxism."

For instance: the coal-mines and all the machinery of the coal-mines and the houses in which the miners live and the stores of food and the clothing, etc., which keep the miners alive while the coal is being mined, that is during the process of production – all these, which now belong to capitalists who make a profit out of the miners' labour, would then belong to the State, which would allot the coal produced to all who needed it. So it would be with all farms, farming

implements, and cattle and horses and the stores of food and clothing and houses necessary to the labourers on the land during the
process of production. So it would be with all stone-quarrying and
timber-felling, and carpentry and brick-making for the continued
production of the houses necessary to the producers during production. So it would be with all corresponding material for making cloth
for clothing. So it would be with everything which was made in the
whole country. The officers of the State would share out the wealth
produced, so that it would be consumed by all the citizens, and there
would be an end to the exploitation of one man by another and to the
uncertainty of living.

Communism is simply that form of Socialism in which all that
is thus shared out by the State would be shared equally, the State
giving every family an equal share in proportion to the numbers of
people which had to be supported in the family, from one upwards.

The reason I have called Communism the logical and only
possible ultimate form of Socialism is that there could be under
Socialism no reason for any other form of distribution.

Some time ago certain Socialists used to try to get out of this
necessity for Communism, so as not to frighten rich people with their
proposals for reform. They would say to a man who was making,
say, £5,000 a year because he owned a lot of capital and land and
had rents and profits coming to him from the work of his labourers:
"You will have just as much under Socialism, for we recognise what
a superior kind of person you are, and when the State shares out its
wealth among its citizens it will give you as much as you have now,
leaving the same difference between rich and poor, only seeing to it
that the poor always at least have enough to live on. Where we give
one ticket to the labourer to claim out of the common stores what he
wants for a week we will give you fifty tickets, so that you will get
fifty times as much if you like." But of course this was nonsense, and
was soon discovered to be nonsense. With everybody working for
the State under orders all would naturally claim equality, and there
would be no way of preventing their getting an equal share except
force. In justice, supposing a Socialist state to arise, there could be
only the Communist form of it.

This scheme has never been put into practice, and when we
look closely at it we shall discover, I think, why it never will be put
into practice.

The reason it cannot be put into practice is this: Although we use the words "the State" this mere idea means in practice real men who act as officials to represent the State. Actual men with their varying characters, good and bad, lazy and industrious, just and unjust, have got to undertake the enormous business *first* of running production in the interest of all, *next* of distributing the resultant wealth equally to all.

Now there are two qualities in man which make action of this sort break down. The first is that men love independence – they like to feel themselves their own masters. They like therefore to *own*, so that they may do what they like with material things. The next is that men like to get as much as possible of good things. Both these feelings are universally true of the human race. You will find exceptional people, of course, who are just as contented with a little as with a great deal, and you will find exceptional people who do not care about independence or about owning, and who are quite willing to be run by other people, or to give up all possession for the sake of some special way of living: that is, there is a comparatively small number of men and women who, in order to live free from responsibility, or in order to devote themselves to religion or to some form of study and contemplation, will give up all property and have the material side of their lives administered for them. But men and women in general will both want to get all they can of good things with the least possible exertion in the getting of them, and they will also desire freedom to exercise their own wills and deal with material objects as they choose.

Now the Socialist scheme requires both these very strong emotions, common to all mankind, to be suppressed. The people who run the State – that is the politicians – are to be absolutely just (although there is no one to force them to be just), they are to forget all personal wishes and to think of nothing but the good of those whose labour they direct and among whom they share out the wealth that is produced. We know by experience that politicians are not angels of this sort. It is absurd to imagine that men coveting public office (and living the life of intrigue necessary to get it) would suddenly turn into unselfish and devoted beings of this ideal kind. You cannot give this enormous power to men without their abusing it.

The second force making against the establishment of Socialism is still stronger. You will never get the run of men and women contented to live their whole lives entirely under orders. In exceptional moments a large part of individual freedom will be given up to the necessity of the State – as during the Great War; for if the State did not survive the individual's life and that of his children would not be worth living. The individual in abnormal crises goes through a great deal of suffering for a moment in order that he and his should have less pain in the long run. But even in such crises a large part of liberty remains to him. Under Socialism he would have none. He would have to do what he was told by his task-masters, much more than even the poorest labourers now have to do what they are told by task-masters. And there would also be this difference: that *everyone* would be in that situation and there would be no way out. Not a part of life, nor so many hours a day, but the whole of life, would be subject to orders given by others. This, humanity would certainly find intolerable.

That is why, I think, Socialism has never been put into practice and never can be put into practice. There have been attempts at it, but even when they are sincere and not the mere product of alien despotism they break down. As in Russia today, where, whether the Jew adventurers who seized power were sincere or mere tyrants, they have, in spite of their attempt at seizing all the soil and keeping the peasants dependent on them, been compelled at last to let nearly all the nation live as owners tilling their own land.

It is no reply to this to say that the State always has owned, and actually can and does own, *some* part of the means of production (such as the Post Office and certain forests and lands here in England, and, abroad, most mountain land, all mines and much else) and direct them with success. The point of Socialism – the one condition necessary to its existence – is that the State should own *all* the means of production that really count. Between the normal exercise of a partial function and the abnormal exercise of a universal function is all the difference between *plus* and *minus*. A partial state ownership working in a society the determining character of which is private ownership is an utterly different thing, even an *opposite* thing to general state ownership determining the character of society and allowing only exceptional private ownership. Socialism can only be (*a*) good (*b*) possible when men desire, and are at ease in, the latter kind of state; that is, desire and are at ease in complete forgetfulness of self coupled with justice as men ruling, and complete surrender of personal honour and freedom and appetite as men ruled.

VI

INTERNATIONAL EXCHANGE

INTERNATIONAL exchange is not really different from the domestic exchanges which go on within a nation. The foreigner who has some product of his own to exchange against a product of ours deals as a private man with other private men, and if you could see all the exchanges of the world going on you would not distinguish between the character of an exchange, say, between Devonshire and London and one between London and the Argentine. The Devonshire man grows wheat, which he sells perhaps in a London market, and buys manufactured products which a merchant in London provides. The farmer in the Argentine does much the same thing, sells wheat and receives in exchange what manufactures he needs, precisely as though he were living in Devonshire instead of abroad. He does not trade with "England," but with a particular merchant or company in England.

But there are certain points about international trade which one must get clear unless one is to make mistakes in the political problems arising out of it.

In the first place, international trade is always subject to a certain interference which domestic trade does not suffer. All countries have a TARIFF, that is, a set of taxes upon a great number of the articles coming in from abroad. Even those countries which, as England did until quite lately, believe in leaving their citizens on equal terms with foreign competitors and have gone in for complete free trade, examine all goods at the port of entry or at special points on the frontier, both in order to raise revenue and to keep out undesirable goods, such as certain drugs; nor does any country allow *all* things to come in unexamined, lest forbidden things should come in unobserved. Moreover, it is important to measure the nature and volume of a nation's foreign trade, and this cannot be done without stopping things at the ports or frontiers and examining them.

In general, international trade differs from domestic trade first of all in this – that it always has to pass through an examination at the frontiers through which it enters. It also differs from domestic trade in that it has to use another currency. Even when all countries have a gold currency, there are certain small fluctuations in the exchange values of the different currencies. For instance: before the war the English pound was worth in gold about 25¼ French francs, but you hardly ever had this "Parity" (as it is called) exact. The franc would fluctuate slightly against the sovereign – sometimes above, sometimes below "Parity" by a penny, or even some times more than a penny, one way or the other. With many countries whose currency was not in a good condition the fluctuations would be more violent, and of course since the war, now that so many nations no longer have a gold currency at all, but a fictitious paper currency, the value of one currency against another fluctuates wildly. Within a year you could get only 50 francs for an English sovereign and then a little later as much as 80 francs.

Within one country exchanges can be simply conducted by counting all values in the currency of the country; but international trade, involving the use of two or more currencies, cannot be so simple.

There is also a third point in international trade which must be understood, and which proceeds from the very fact that international exchanges do not essentially differ from the exchanges which take place within the same country, and that is the fact that exchanges are not simple contracts between two parties, but follow a whole chain of contracts, covering a great number of parties.

We saw, in the first part of this book, that exchange even within one country was not simple barter but Multiple Exchange.

In domestic exchange a farmer sells his wheat to a broker, but does not purchase a lorry from the same buyer: he receives money from the buyer, and with that money buys a lorry, say, a month later. But what has really happened is a whole chain of exchanges in between the wheat and the lorry – a miller has bought the wheat from the broker, a baker the flour from the miller, and so on until towards the end of the chain a caster has sold castings to a motor maker who has assembled them and sold the lorry to the farmer.

It is the same with international exchanges; as we saw in the earlier part of this book. There is an international chain of exchanges.

The total number of units engaged in this international chain may be as large as you like; there may be ten or fifty or a hundred links before it is complete. But the universal principle holds that imports and exports usually balance. Whatever you import from abroad into a country you must, as a general rule, pay for by exporting an equivalent set of values created within your own country. But there are certain exceptions to this rule which are sometimes lost sight of.

In the first place, the imports and the exports need not all be what are called "visible" imports and exports. Many of them may be, and some always are, "invisible." The most obvious example of these are "freights," that is, sums paid for the carriage of goods between one country and another. Thus, in the old days before the war you would find England importing more than she exported, and one of the principal reasons for the difference was that the imports were mostly brought in English ships. Thus if a man in the Argentine were sending 50 tons of wheat to England worth £500, England, after a long chain of trade with many countries, including the Argentine, would be exporting values against this £500 worth of wheat, which would be worth, say, not £500, but only £450. The difference of £50 was made up by the cost of bringing the wheat from the Argentine to England *in an English ship*. In other words, £50 worth of the total £500 worth of wheat stood for the sum which the man in the Argentine had to pay to the English sailors to bring his wheat over the sea.

Further, a wealthy or strong country very often levied tribute upon a poorer or weaker one, and this tribute might take several forms. There was the tribute of interest upon loans. If English bankers had lent to people in Egypt a million pounds with interest at forty thousand pounds a year Egyptian production would have to export to England, either directly or roundabout through the chain of trade, forty thousand pounds' worth of goods, against which England had not to send out anything.

Another form of tribute – though a small one – is that paid in pensions. A man having worked all his life in the Civil Service in India (for instance) would retire upon a yearly pension of a thousand pounds a year; but this pension was levied upon the taxpayers of India, and if the man came to live in England and spent his pension there – as nearly all of them did – it meant that India had to export a thousand pounds' worth of goods every year to England, against which England sent nothing back.

In the same way the shareholder in some works or firms situated in a foreign country would, if he lived in England, cause an import to come in equivalent to his dividends or profits, and against that England would send out nothing.

But the point to remember is, that *the mere volume of trade* (that is, the total of things imported and of things exported) *is no indication of the wealth or prosperity of the country importing and exporting.*

A country may be very wealthy, although it is doing hardly any international trade, because it may be producing within its own boundaries a great deal of wealth of a kind sufficient to nearly all, or all, its needs. Again, of international trade (and it is exceedingly important to remember this, because most people go wrong on it) *nothing increases the wealth of a country except the imports.*

It ought to be quite clear, especially in the case of an island like Great Britain, that it *loses* what it sends out and *gains* what it brings in. Yet people get muddled about even this very simple proposition, because the individual trader thinks of his transactions as an individual sale. He does not consider the nature of trade as a whole. The individual trader, for instance, who makes locomotives and exports them, gets paid, let us say, £10,000 for each locomotive. In point of fact this means that in the long run he or someone else in England will exercise £10,000 worth of demand for foreign goods. But the individual trader does not usually think of that; he thinks only of his own transactions, and he would be very much surprised if he were told that his sending the locomotive abroad was, *regarded in itself, and apart from the import which it assumed,* a loss to the country of £10,000 worth of wealth.

You often hear people in political arguments talking as though the falling off of exports from a country were a bad thing and the increase of imports also a bad thing. It cannot be so in the long run. The excess of imports over exports is the national profit on the whole of its foreign transactions, and any country which is exporting regularly more than it imports is paying tribute to foreigners abroad, while every country which regularly imports more than it exports is receiving tribute.

Of course, if you consider only a short period of time, the falling off of exports may be a bad sign; for it may mean that the corresponding imports will not be gathered. If in this country we saw our exports regularly falling year by year we should be right to take alarm, for this would almost certainly mean that a corresponding falling off in imports would sooner or later take place also, and that therefore our total wealth would be diminished. But considered over a sufficient space of time, it is obvious that the excess of imports over exports is a gain and that the excess of exports over imports is a loss.

One last thing to remember about international trade is that the very different importance of foreign trade to different countries makes the foreign politics of nations differ equally. A country which can supply itself with all it needs is free to risk its foreign trade for some other issue. A country importing its necessities cannot risk the loss of such trade, for it is a matter of life and death. The United States is in the first position. It has within its own boundaries not only all the minerals it needs, but also all the petrol and all the raw material for making cloth, and all the leather for boots, and all the rest of it. But a country like England is in quite a different position. We only grow half the meat we need and about one-fifth of the corn. Therefore it is absolutely necessary for us to have a foreign trade. If all the foreign trade of the United States were to be destroyed tomorrow, the United States, though somewhat poorer, would still be very rich and able to carry on without the help of anyone else. But if our foreign trade were destroyed there would be a terrible famine and most of us would die.

Nations differ very much in this respect, but of all nations Great Britain is that which is most vitally interested in maintaining a great foreign trade, and next after Great Britain Belgium is similarly interested, for Belgium also needs to import four-fifths of its bread-stuffs. Almost every country except the United States *must* have some foreign trade if it is to live normally. For instance: France, though largely a self-sufficing country, has no petrol. It has to buy its petrol abroad and must export goods to pay for that import. Nor has it quite enough coal for its needs, and, before the war, it had not nearly enough iron. Italy has no coal, no petrol and no iron to speak of – not nearly enough for its needs. And so it is with pretty well every nation in Europe. But of all nations our own and Belgium – our own particularly – are in the most need of maintaining a large foreign trade.

This affects all our policy, it is the root of both the greatness and peril of England. It also tends to make English people judge the wealth of foreigners by the volume of their trade, and that is a great error.

VII

FREE TRADE AND PROTECTION
AS POLITICAL ISSUES

IN this matter of international trade there rose up, about a hundred years ago, a great political discussion in England between what was called "Free Trade" and what was called "Protection."

This discussion is still going on and affecting the life of the country, and it is important to understand the principles of it, for we have here one of the chief applications of theoretical Political Economy to actual conditions.

I dealt with this subject briefly in the first part of this book under "Elementary Principles," but I return to it here in more detail because it has given rise, in political application, to the most important economic discussion in modern England.

The Free Traders were those who said that England would be wealthier, as a whole, if there were no restriction upon exchange at all, whether internal or external. A man having something to exchange with his English neighbour was, of course, free to exchange it without any interference; but the Free Trader's particular point was that a man having something to exchange with a *foreign* purchaser should be equally free to exchange it, without any interference at the ports in the way of export duty taxing the transaction. In the same way he said that the foreigner should be perfectly free to send here any goods he had to exchange against ours, and should neither be kept out by laws nor restricted by special import duties at the ports.

"In this way," said the Free Traders, "we shall get the maximum of wealth for the whole country."

The Protectionists, on the other hand, said: "Here are a lot of people engaged on a particular form of production in England.

Those who have their capital in it are making profits, those who own the land on which the capital is invested are getting rents, and the working people are getting wages. The foreigner, having special advantages for this kind of production, which make him able to produce this particular thing more cheaply than we can, brings in that cheaper produce and offers it for sale to Englishmen. The people to whom it is offered for sale will, of course, buy the foreign stuff because it is cheaper. The result will be that the English people who have invested their capital in producing this particular thing – that is, who have got implements together and buildings, and the rest, suitable for producing this thing – will be ruined. It will not be worth their while to go on, for no one will buy their goods. Their profits will be extinguished, and their capital will decay to nothing. The rents on the land they occupy will also disappear, and, what is worst of all, the large population which live on wages produced by this kind of work will starve or have to be supported, idle, by other people. Their power of producing wealth will be lost to England. Therefore, let us tax this cheap foreign import so that our production at home shall be *protected*. Let us tax the foreign goods as they come in, so that the cost of producing abroad, with this tax added, comes to at least as much as the cost of producing the same stuff at home. In this way it will still be worth while for our people at home to go on producing this kind of thing. The Englishman at home will be just as ready to buy his fellow citizen's produce as the foreigner's, for the price of each will be the same."

The Protectionist even said: "Let us make this tariff so high that the foreign goods are sold at a *dis*advantage – that is, let the tax on the foreign goods be such that, added to the cost of production abroad, they cannot be sold in England save at a *higher* price than the English goods. In this way only the English goods will be bought here and the home industry will flourish as it did before."

Such were the two political theories, standing one against the other.

Now let us look into the economic principles underlying these two opposing parties, and see which of them had the best of the argument.

We have already seen, in the first part of this book, the elementary economic principle that Exchange is only the last stage in the process of production.

And we have also had fixed the principle that *freedom of exchange tends to produce a maximum of wealth within the area to which it applies,* and that interference with freedom of exchange tends to reduce the total possible wealth of that area. This is so obvious that all the great modern nations are careful to let exchange be as free as possible *within their own boundaries.*

Goods can be freely exchanged without interference all over the United States and all over Great Britain and all over France, etc., because if you were to set up tolls and interferences with exchange *within* the country the total wealth of the country would necessarily be diminished.

Now the Free Traders extended this principle to foreign trade. They said: "If the foreigner comes to us with something which he can sell to us cheaper than we can make it ourselves that is an advantage to us, and it is short-sighted to interfere with it under the idea that we are benefiting the existing trade which is threatened by foreign competition. For it means that we are producing something with difficulty which we could get with much less work if we turned our attention to things which we can produce with ease. Or, again, it means that with the same amount of work devoted to things we make well and exchange against the foreigner's goods we shall get much more of the things which the foreigner can make more easily than we can."

If we take a concrete example we shall see what the Free Traders' argument means.

Supposing people in this country had never heard of foreign wine, but had to make their wine out of their own grapes grown in hot-houses, and at great expense, the wine coming, let us say, to £1 a gallon. Meanwhile we are producing easily great quantities of coal because we have great coal-mines near the surface. We come to hear of people living in another climate who can grow grapes easily in the open, who need much less labour and capital to ripen them than we do in our artificial way in hot-houses, and who can therefore send us wine at 10s. a gallon. Then we can get for each £1 worth of labour and capital twice as much wine as we got before. Instead of wasting our time artificially growing grapes in hot-houses to make our wine, let the people who used to work in the hot-houses become coal-miners, so that more coal may be produced and this extra coal exchanged for foreign wine. A pound's worth of labour and capital in coal will get us 2 gallons of wine from the foreigner when the same amount of labour and capital used in making the wine ourselves would only get us one gallon. Let the capital that used to keep up the hot-houses be spent in developing mines, and we shall find as a result that we are as rich as ever we used to be in coal and richer in wine. Our total wealth will be increased.

In the particular case of the English dispute about Free Trade and Protection not wine but a much more important thing was concerned, namely food; and that was what gave the political discussion its practical value and made it so violent. It is also because food was in question that the Free Traders won, and that England was, for a whole lifetime, up to the Great War, a Free Trade country – that is, a country allowing all foreign produce to come in and compete on equal terms with home produce.

This country, at the beginning of the discussion a hundred years ago, was already producing great quantities of manufactured goods: cloth and machinery, ships and so on. It also produced on its fields the wheat and meat and dairy produce with which it fed itself. But as the population increased the amount of food being produced on the soil of England, though getting larger in the total, got smaller in proportion to the rapidly increasing population. Therefore there was a danger of its getting dearer. The Free Traders said: "Let foreign food come in free. If it is produced in climates where for the same amount of labour you can get more wheat and more meat and more dairy produce then, of course, many of our agricultural people will have to give up working on the land. But they can take to manufacturing, and the total amount of food which the English will get for so much labour on their part will be greater. Where an agricultural labourer working an hour, for instance, can get a pound's weight of food, the same man working one hour in a factory will get, say, by exchange of the manufacture against foreign food, two pounds of food, if we allow all foreign food to come in free."

These Free Trade arguments look, when they are first stud-
ied, not only simple and clear, but unanswerable, and indeed most
educated men – nearly all educated men – in Queen Victoria's reign,
thought they *were* unanswerable, and that Protectionists here at home
(who were no longer allowed to put their theories into laws) and Protectionists abroad who had kept up tariffs against foreign trade, were
simply ignorant and foolish men who did not properly understand
the elements of Economic Science.

To see whether the Free Traders were right or wrong in these
ideas, let us next turn to the arguments with which the Protectionists
met them.

These arguments were of two kinds:—

(*a*) There were Protectionists who said: "We cannot follow all
these elaborate abstract discussions about a science called 'Economics'; we are practical men with plenty of common sense and experience, and all we know is that if the foreigner comes in free we shall be
ruined. He can sell his wheat at such a price that our farmers will lose
on it. Our labourers will leave the land, the rents paid to our landlords will vanish. You will thus ruin English wealth altogether."

(*b*) There was another kind of Protectionist who said: "You
Free Traders take for granted, and depend upon, one capital point, to
wit, *that the labour now employed in a particular form of production, and
the capital employed in it, both of which will be destroyed by Free Trade,
can be used more profitably in some other form of Production.* But we, the
Protectionists, say that, in the particular case in question, they would
not be used more profitably. We say that, in point of fact, things being
as they are, the national character being what it is, the arrangements
of our English society and its traditions being what we know them
to be, the ruined industry will go on getting worse and worse, artificially supported by relief from the community outside it, the farmer
losing year after year and still hanging on, the land going back to
weeds and marsh, the buildings falling down, and so forth. *We* say
that, though it may theoretically be possible to use in other ways the
labour and capital thus displaced, in practice you will destroy more
wealth than you will create."

These two kinds of arguments on the Protectionist side are still
to be heard everywhere today.

It ought to be perfectly clear to anyone who thinks about the matter at all that argument (*a*) was nonsense, for people and capital driven out of an industry ill-suited to our present conditions are not thereby destroyed. They may very well find employment producing more total wealth in another. But argument (*b*) was a good argument *if the statement about the impossibility of changing from one trade to another were in practice true.* The whole discussion really turned upon the last point.

Unfortunately for the Protectionists, those who defended their cause in this country nearly all used argument (*a*), and were very properly derided as fools by the Free Traders. Argument (*b*) was only used by a comparatively small number of thoughtful men and they were under this disadvantage – that they were arguing with regard to a possible or probable future with no past experience to guide them, and that many years must pass before it could be discovered whether, in practice, what they said was true or false; whether in practice the ruin of English agriculture would diminish the well-being of England as a whole or not.

Further, the population continued to increase at a great rate, and that all in the towns and on the coal-fields. Our manufacturing productions went up and up and up, the total wealth of the country enormously increased, and these processes hid and made to seem insignificant the corresponding decay of the fields. We had no need for Protection in any domestic manufactured goods; we had begun to use coal before anybody else; we had developed machinery before anybody else. The only thing which there could be any point in protecting was agriculture, and that would have meant dearer food for the wage-earners in the towns.

The great consequence was that Free Trade won hands down, and for a long time all its opponents, however distinguished or reasonable, were laughed at.

But if we wish to be worthy students of Economic Science we cannot dismiss the quarrel so simply. There is such a thing as a strong *economic* argument in favour of Protection in particular circumstances. The practical proof of this truth is the immense increase in wealth which took place in the German Empire during the thirty years before the Great War, which increase exactly corresponded with a highly protective tariff. The same thing happened in the United States at the same time. But the theoretical argument in favour of Protection is much better, because the increase of wealth in Germany and the United States under Protection might be due to other causes, whilst it can be shown by *reason* that Protection itself, in particular cases, increases the total national wealth. With the proof of this I will end the present chapter.

We have seen that the following formula is true:— "Freedom of exchange tends to increase the total amount of wealth of all that area which it covers."

But what gives the argument for Protection, in special cases, its value is, as we saw on page 67, a second formula equally true. Though freedom of exchange tends to increase the total wealth of an area over which it extends, *yet it does not tend to increase the wealth of every part of that area.* Therefore, if a part of the area over which freedom of exchange extends finds itself impoverished by the process, it may be enriched by interfering with freedom of exchange over the boundaries of its own special part.

Therein lies the whole argument for Protection in particular cases.

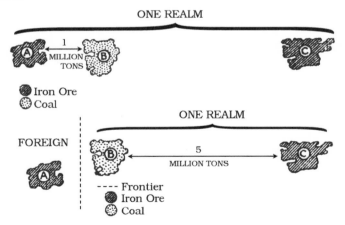

Let us take for example three islands, two close together and one far away, and prove the case by figures.

We will number them A, B, C. Island A is full of iron ore. Island B is full of coal. Island C is also full of iron ore, like Island A, but it is a long way off.

Iron ore naturally comes to the coal area to be smelted, because, being heavier, it can be carried in smaller bulk. It is cheaper to bring iron ore to coal than coal to iron ore. If all three islands belong to the same realm what will happen is quite clear. Island B will import iron ore from Island A and will smelt it and turn it into pig-iron and steel and iron manufactures of all kinds, while Island C, a long way off, will remain unused. We will suppose the climate of No. C to be bleak, the soil bad, and the people there, since they cannot sell their iron ore on account of the distance at which they stand, make a very poor livelihood out of grazing a few cattle.

Let us suppose that the amount of iron ore imported every year by Island B from Island A is worth £10 million. This of course has to be paid for. In other words, Island B has got to export manufactured goods in iron and steel back to Island A as payment for the iron ore which Island B imports for smelting. It also has to pay for the freight on the iron ore from Island A, that is, for the cost of bringing it over the sea to Island B. Let us suppose this cost to be one million. The total value of the iron goods produced on Island B, after being smelted with the coal of Island B, is, let us say, £30 million. Of this, £11 million goes back for the cost of carrying the ore from Island A and for its purchase. Meanwhile we may neglect economic values of Island C, because the few wretched inhabitants and their handful of cattle hardly count.

Here, then, we have a wealth of £30,000,000 in manufactured iron goods, of which £10,000,000 goes to Island A and £19,000,000 to Island B, and £1 million to whoever carries the ore in ships. If you were estimating the wealth of the whole realm made up of the three islands, A, B and C, you would say: "The wealth of these people consists in manufactured iron and steel goods. It is equivalent to £30,000,000 a year, of which some £10,000,000 is revenue to Island A and £19,000,000 is revenue to Island B and £1 million earned in freights. The wealth of Island C is negligible." Well and good.

Now supposing the political conditions to change. Islands B and C belong to one realm in future but Island A has become a foreigner. The realm to which Islands B and C belong turns Protectionist and sets up a barrier in the shape of a tariff against iron ore coming from abroad. We have seen that the cost of carrying iron ore from Island

A to Island B was £1,000,000. Island C being much farther away from Island B, let us say that the cost of carrying is £5,000,000, but it is carried by subjects of the realm. The tariff put up by the realm to which Island B and C belong is what is called "prohibitive" – that is, it is so high that it keeps the iron ore of Island A out altogether, and the smelters on Island B are bound to get their iron ore from that distant Island C. Let us see what happens.

Island B has now got to pay a freight, that is, cost of bringing the iron ore, five times as much as it used to be. Instead of paying £11,000,000 for its ore (£10,000,000 at the mine and £1,000,000 for carriage) it is now paying £15,000,000 (£10,000,000 at the mine and £5,000,000 for carriage). It still makes £30,000,000 worth of goods a year, but it only has £15,000,000 left over for its own income, instead of the £19,000,000 which it used to have. It is thus impoverished.

But Island C, from having hardly any income at all, has now an income of £10,000,000 a year. Island A is ruined. Protection has put the getting of the ore under unnatural conditions. It has compelled the coal-owners to go much farther off for their ore than they need have done under Free Trade. The total wealth of all three islands altogether is less than it used to be by £4,000,000, for they are adding £4,000,000 extra to the cost of getting the raw material. *But the total combined wealth of B and C, even if they pay foreign ships to bring the ore, is now greater than it used to be under the old Free Trade.* Island B has £15,000,000; Island C has £10,000,000 – the total is £25,000,000. If they pay their own sailors to bring the ore it is £30,000,000. Under the old conditions the total of B and C alone was only £19,000,000. Island A is ruined and the total wealth of the whole system is less, but the Protectionists of the realm, which now only includes B and C, are quite indifferent to that. They are thinking of the wealth of their common country, and are indifferent to the ruin of others, and their policy is *increasing* the wealth of their common country at the expense of foreigners.

In that example lies the argument for Protection. *If Island C could do something other than mine ore, if it had other forms of wealth, or by ingenuity or luck could discover some new fields in which its activities might develop, then the argument for Protection in this case would break down.* Island B would say: "Let me get my iron ore cheap from the foreigner in Island A, and do you, on Island C, develop (let us say) dairy farming, or something else which I cannot do and which Island B cannot do. In that way we shall all three benefit, and the common realm, consisting of Island B and Island C, will be richer than ever. Island B will have all its old profit of £19,000,000 (instead of being reduced to £15,000,000), and Island C can well develop a dairy produce of more than £7,000,000."

One ought to be able to see quite clearly from an example like this how true it is that *the argument in favour of Protection applies to particular cases only, and turns entirely upon whether an undeveloped part of the energies of the community can be turned into new channels or not.*

We have an excellent, though small, example to hand in England today. The English people have to send abroad about £4 worth of goods every year per family for pig-meat, that is, bacon and hams and the rest. There is no reason why they should do this. They could produce the pigs on their own farms without drawing a single person from the factories and keep this mass of manufactured goods for their own use. The reason we are in this state in the matter of pig-meat is that our agriculture has generally got into such a hole that people will not bestir themselves to produce enough pigs. So here is a definite case in point, and only experiment could show whether Protection would pay here or would not pay.

Protection ought to take the form of saying:—

"Any pig-meat from abroad must pay such and such a sum per pound at the ports as it enters." This would raise the price of pig-meat in England somewhat. If it raised the price to such an amount that the English people as a whole had to pay £2 more a family, *and if at that increased rate of price agricultural people could be stimulated into feeding the right amount of pigs and taking the necessary trouble to keep the supply going,* then the total wealth of the community would be increased £2 per family. Even if the price had to increase till each family on the average paid £3 more, or £3 10s. 0d. more, it would still be of advantage to the nation *on condition that the higher price really did make the farmers breed enough pigs, without lessening their production of other things.* But if, when the charge on the community had risen to £4 per family, it did not stimulate the production of pigs in this country sufficiently to supply the market, then your protection of pigs would be run at a loss.

VIII

BANKING

DURING the last two hundred and fifty years there has arisen, among other modern economic institutions, the institution of BANKING.

It has origins much older; indeed, people did something of the kind at *all* times, but "Banking" as a fully developed institution grew up in this comparatively short time: since the middle of the seventeenth century. It began in Holland and England and spread to other countries.

Like other modern institutions, it only became really important in the latter half of this period, that is, during the last hundred years or so; quite recently – in the last fifty years – it has become of such supreme importance by the mastery it has got over the whole commonwealth that everybody ought to try to understand its character. The power of the banks comes today into the lives of all of us and largely affects the relations between different nations. Indeed, it has become so powerful quite lately that one of the principal things we have to watch in politics is the enmity which the power of the banks has aroused and the way in which that power is being attacked.

The essential of Banking lies in these two combined ideas: (1) that a man will leave his money in custody of another man when that other man has better opportunities for keeping it safe than he has; (2) that the money so left in custody *may* be used by the custodian of the money without the real owner being very anxious what is being done with it, so long as he is certain to get it when he wants it.

The putting together of these two ideas – which are ideas naturally arising in everybody's mind – is the origin of all Banking, and the moral basis upon which Banking reposes.

A man has £1,000 in gold. He has to travel or to go abroad on a war, or is not certain of the safety of so large a sum if it is kept in his house. He therefore gives it into the custody of a man whom he can trust, and who, on account of special circumstances, can keep it more securely than he himself can. What the owner of the £1,000 wants in the transaction is to be certain of getting a part or the whole of his money whenever he may need it. He does not want the individual pieces of money. So long as he can get the value of them *or of part of them* at any moment from the man to whom he gave custody of the original sum, he is satisfied.

A good many other people feel the same necessity. The man who has special opportunities for looking after *all* their sums of money collects them together and has them in his strong box in safe keeping. Those who have acted thus would be very angry if they found their money had been lost, or that when they came to ask for £20 or £100 out of their thousand pounds – needing such a sum for the transactions of the moment – the man in whose custody the whole lay was unable to let them have the £20 or £100 required. But so long as the *depositor* (as he is called, that is, the man who hands over his money for safe custody) finds himself, in practice, always getting the whole or any part of his deposit on demand, he is content; *and will not be annoyed to find that the person in whose custody he left the money has been using it in the meantime.*

For instance: I might leave £1,000 in gold in the custody of someone who is better able than I to prevent its being stolen. I am saved all the trouble of looking after it, and I can call on a part of it or all of it whenever I like. If there were only myself leaving it thus with one friend, and it was a particular transaction between us two, that friend would be acting wrongly if he were to take my £1,000 and buy a ship with it, say, and do trade. No doubt he would earn a profit, and could say to me when I came back for £100 of it: "I am sorry that I cannot give you your £100, but I have used the money, without telling you, to buy a ship. The ship will earn a profit of £200 at the end of the year, and then you can have back your £100 if you like, and if you press me, I will even sell the ship and you shall have back the whole of your £1,000."

In that case I should naturally answer: "No one gave you leave to use my money. You have embezzled it, and you have acted like a thief."

But when a very great number of men entrust their money in this fashion, and do not specially stipulate that it should be left untouched, when there is a sort of silent understanding that, if whenever they want it, the money will be forthcoming, then they do not ask too closely what has been done with the whole of the sum in the custodian's hands. For if *very many* people are thus "banking" their money with one safe custodian, only a certain proportion will *at any one time* want their money, and the rest can be used without danger of the "banker's" failing to meet any particular demand. Thus, Banking, that is, the use of other peoples' money, arises and becomes a natural process because it is of mutual advantage. The banker can earn profits with that average amount of money which always remains in his hands; the depositors have their money safely looked after and may even share in the profit.

A hundred men, let us say, have given £1,000 each into the hands of such a custodian, who has come to be called their "banker." The total sum of money in this man's hands is £100,000. It is found in practice, over the average of a number of years, that this hundred men do not "draw" upon (that is, ask for their money to be paid out to them) their banker more than to the extent of, let us say, £100 every month each, and it is also found that, while they need this £100 to pay wages or bills or what not, they also come back with the money they earn (say, £120 per month, on the average) and give it back to their banker for safe keeping. In several years of this practice the banker discovers that he must have about 100 times £100, that is £10,000, in free cash to meet the demands upon him, and that he gets rather more put into his custody in the same period of a month, year in and year out. It follows that he always has about £90,000 in gold doing nothing the whole time. He says to himself: "Why should I not use this money to buy instruments of production – ships or ploughs, or machinery or what not – and produce more wealth? It will not hurt those who have deposited it with me, for I have found that, *on the average,* they never want more than a tenth of their money out at the same time (and they are also perpetually paying in more money to me – so that they and I are quite safe), and if I make a good profit by the use of the things I shall have bought with this £90,000 I can offer them part of the profit. So we are both benefited."

That is what the banker began by doing at the very origins of this institution of Banking. It was a little odd. It was not quite straightforward. But the depositors, most of them, knew what was going on, and at any rate did not protest. And if, when a profit was made out of their combined money, they got some of that profit, they were glad enough to see that their money had been put to some use and that they had become richer by its use; while if they had kept it to themselves in scattered small amounts it would not have made them any richer.

In England we can trace the origins of a great many banks, and of the fortunes of their owners, proceeding along these lines. For instance: there was a family of silversmiths rather more than two hundred years ago. They had a shop in which silver objects were bought and sold, and they also had gold plate to buy and sell. They had strong-boxes in which these things were kept, and they paid money to men who guarded these strong-boxes. It was a natural thing for people to go to this shop and say: "I have here a thousand pounds in gold which is not very safe at home. Will you look after it for me, on condition of course that I may call for any amount of it when I want it; and what will you charge for your trouble?" The silversmiths said: "Yes, we will do this, we will charge nothing," and in that way they got hold of very large sums which people left with them. They found, as we have just seen, that in practice, year after year, only a certain amount of the sums were required of them at any one time, and rather than leave the big balance lying idle they used it for buying useful things which would produce more wealth. They lent the money sometimes to the State for its purposes, that is, to the King of the time. Sometimes they employed it in other ways which earned a profit. The people who left the money with them always found that they could get back whatever they wanted when they asked for it, and they were content. That is how Banking arose.

Another example of which I know the history and which is very interesting is that of a squire in the West of England who lived rather less than two hundred years ago and has given his name to one of our great banks still existing today. This squire was a rich man who had many friends coming to his table. He had the reputation of good judgment and his friends would say: "I will leave this sum of money in your custody," for they knew that he would be able to put it to good use and give them part of the profit. Thus, looking after the money of neighbours, he came to look after the money of a great many people whom his neighbours recommended, and at last had hundreds of "clients," as the phrase went – that is, of people who would leave their money with him, knowing that he would earn a profit both for himself and for them; at the same time the money would be safely kept, and they might call for a portion of it whenever they wanted it.

From such origins the Banking System gradually extended until, about a hundred years ago, or rather more, every rich family in this country had a considerable sum of money left at a bank, and paid into the banker's coffers further sums of money which they received. Each had a book of accounts with the bank showing exactly how much had been put in and therefore how much they could "draw" upon. At first the clients, or depositors, would "draw" some portion of their money which they might immediately need by way of a letter. Thus, if their banker's name was Mr. Smith, they would write this note: "To Mr. Smith. Please pay my servant who brings this letter £20 out of the £1,000 which I left with you the other day." They would sign this letter and send the servant with it; the banker would give the £20 to the servant and the servant would give a receipt against it.

That was the origin of what are nowadays called "cheques." The letter giving authority for the messenger to draw the money grew more and more formal and was drawn up more and more in the same terms to save trouble. Then the bankers would have the forms printed, so that the client who wanted to draw would have the least possible trouble. If you look at a cheque today you will see that it is nothing but the old letter put into the simplest terms. At the head of the cheque is the name of the bank; then there is the word "Pay," and after that the client adds the sum which he wants paid and signs his name to prove that it is really he who is entitled to have the sum and who is asking for it. The words "or bearer" are sometimes printed after the word "Pay," so that anyone bringing the cheque for the client can get the money for him.

But to prevent people using these pieces of paper to get money without having the right to it the word "order" was more often substituted for the word "bearer"; and this word "order" means that the owner, who is drawing his money out, says: "Do not pay it to me; pay it to this other person whom I desire to receive the money and whose name I have mentioned above, who will sign to show that *his* order for payment has been met."

For instance: I have £1,000 deposited with my banker, Mr. Smith. I write a letter: "Pay £20 to John Jones *or order.*" This means: "Do not, dear Mr. Smith, send the money back to me, but give it to Mr. Jones who will bring this letter with him, or, if he cannot come himself, will send a signed letter *order* that it should be paid to him." At the beginning of the system, Mr. Jones, to whom I gave the cheque, would write a little letter saying: "Dear Mr. Smith, Mr. So-and-So, who banks with you, has given me the accompanying letter by which I can get £20 of his *by my order.* I therefore send you this letter to tell you that whoever brings this cheque bears my order to give the money to him." He signs the letter "John Jones" and the banker hands over the money to whomever it may be that brings the letter for John Jones.

In process of time the thing was simplified. In place of the letter came the shortened form, the cheque, and you wrote: "Pay £20 to John Jones or order," and John Jones, instead of sending a letter signed by himself, merely put his signature at the back of the cheque. This was called "endorsement," which is a Latin form of the English meaning "putting one's name on the back of anything." A cheque "endorsed" with the name "John Jones," that is, with John Jones's name signed on the back of it, was paid by the bank to whomever John Jones might send to receive the payment. My cheque asking for £20 to be paid to John Jones having fulfilled its object, and the £20 being paid to whomever John Jones had sent after he had "endorsed" that cheque, the cheque was said to have been "honoured" by the bank. The word "honoured" meant that the bank had admitted that I had the money banked with them, and that they were bound to hand it over on seeing my signature asking that it should be handed over.

The convenience of cheques used in this way for business was obvious. If I owed a man £20 and I had £1,000 with my banker, instead of having to draw out twenty sovereigns myself and take them to him, all I had to do was to write out a cheque to the order of this man, who would endorse it and get the money.

Now as Banking grew and came to deal with more and more people, it was probable that this man, Jones, would have a banking account too with somebody. If Mr. Smith was not his banker, then Mr. Brown would be. As we have seen, people not only drew out money from the original sum they had deposited at the bank, they also paid in money as they got it, on account of the convenience of having it looked after safely. So when John Jones got my cheque for £20, he often did not get the actual cash from my banker, Mr. Smith, but simply gave in the cheque, endorsed by him, to Mr. Brown, *his* banker, and said: "Get this from Mr. Smith the other banker, and add it to the sum which I have banked with you, Mr. Brown." The banker Brown did this, and the cheque which I had originally signed in favour of John Jones, having gone the rounds, was sent back to me to prove that the transaction was complete.

As Banking continued to grow this system took on a vast extension. Thousands and thousands of people paid, and were paid, by cheques, of which only a small part were turned into cash, and of which much the greater part were paid into the bankers' offices and then settled by the bankers among themselves.

After many years of this system it became apparent that the enormous transactions, thousands of cheques all crossing each other daily in hundreds of ways, could be simplified by the establishment of what came to be called the "Clearing House."

Thus, suppose three bankers – Mr. Smith, Mr. Brown and Mr. Robinson. I bank with Mr. Smith, and sign a cheque in favour of Mr. Jones who banks with Mr. Brown, because I owe Jones a bill which I can thus pay. I also sign a cheque in favour of Mr. Harding (that is, to the order of Mr. Harding), to whom I also owe money. He banks with Mr. Robinson. Meanwhile Harding perhaps owes money to Jones and pays him a cheque ordering Mr. Robinson (Harding's banker) to pay Jones a sum of money. Jones hands this over to his banker, Mr. Brown. At the end of a certain time – say, a month – the three bankers, Smith, Brown and Robinson, get together and compare the various cheques they have received. It is obvious that a great many will cancel out.

For instance: I have given Jones a cheque for £20 which Mr. Smith, my banker, has to pay to Mr. Brown, Jones's banker. But Mr. Brown has a cheque of Mr. Harding's asking Mr. Robinson to pay £20 to Jones, and Jones has given that to Brown too. Meanwhile

Jones has given me a cheque later on, for something which he owed me, of £10. The bankers compare notes and see that Smith need not pay £20 to Brown, and then ask Brown for £10. It is simpler to pay the difference only. Mr. Smith hands to Mr. Brown what is called the "balance." The difference between £10 and £20 is £10, and Brown hands over £10 to Smith. At the end of another month perhaps it is Robinson, Harding's banker, who finds that on comparing notes he has a balance against him of £10 to Brown: and so on.

When dozens of bankers came to be established with thousands of clients, or "depositors," the convenience of this system was overwhelming. There would perhaps be in a week as many as 10,000 cheques out, and instead of having to make 10,000 separate transactions of paying from Brown to Smith, Smith to Robinson, Robinson back to Brown, and so on, through dozens of bankers, the cheques were compared and only the balances were paid over – or, as the phrase goes, "cleared."

The Clearing House was the place where all the cheques of different banks were put in at regular intervals and compared one with another, so as to see what balances remained over, owing by particular bankers to others.

Meanwhile, as the Banking System grew, most of the ready money in the community came into the hands of the bankers. There was a perpetual coming and going, and paying in and paying out, but there was always among the bankers as a community a very large sum of money lying untouched, a sort of reservoir. It was nearly always very much more than two-thirds of the whole amount which the banks could be called on to pay. That is, the depositors never wanted a third of their deposits out at any one time. The art of a banker, therefore, consisted in knowing how to purchase with this idle money left in their hands fruitful objects for producing future wealth, in other words, "investing" it in "capital enterprises," but always prudently keeping a large reserve ready to meet any demands which their depositors might suddenly make upon them.

So far so good. The Banking System up to this point in its development was an advantage to the community and to individuals. It enabled a large number of small sums which could not be used very well separately to be collected together for big enterprises.

A thousand people, depositing a thousand pounds each, left a million pounds in the hands of the bankers, of which much more than half a million could be used at any time for "development," that is, for buying instruments with which to develop natural resources. The nation would be richer if a deep shaft were sunk and coal were got out of the earth, but it would cost half a million to make that mine. No one of the thousand small depositors could have undertaken such a task: the bank, using all their monies together, could undertake it – and did so.

The Banking System thus rapidly increased the wealth of the country, and that was all to the good. People meanwhile felt their money to be secure, and they had the great advantage of being able to draw cheques for payments they had to make to those to whom they owed money, and of receiving cheques for money due to them instead of perpetually handling and carrying about large sums in metal – the whole passing through the bank and helping to keep this reservoir of wealth perpetually filled and available for use in investment.

That state of affairs lasted to within the memory of men now living, and, as I have said, the Banking System during that time was an advantage to everybody. There was nothing to be said against it.

But then came (as there comes upon every human institution after a certain time) a further phase of development, in which the institution of Banking produced certain perils and evils. Those perils and evils are increasing, and are producing the antagonism to the banks and to their power which everybody is beginning to express today, all over Europe and America, and which we must understand if we are to follow modern political economy. I will show you how these evils in the Banking System arose.

A man having £1,000 in the bank could draw upon it up to the total amount. He could sign a cheque for £100 and then for £500 (making £600) and then for another £400. Supposing he put nothing in during that time, he would have exhausted the whole of what he had in his bank; he would have come to an end of what is called, in the terms of banking, his "balance." There, you might think, was an end of his power to draw cheques. He had got back all his money, so the bank and he had nothing more to do with each other. At first, of course, that was the regular state of affairs. A man could draw out all that he had in the bank, but no more. It seems common sense.

But the banks had plenty of other people's money lying about which had not been drawn out, and much of which had not yet been invested in capital enterprises, such as mining, or what not. They would say to the man who had once put £1,000 into their hands and who had now drawn it all out: "You still want to carry on your business; but you have exhausted all the money you had with us. You will probably want to borrow some money to tide you over until the time when further sums begin to come in to you through what you sell in your business. We are prepared to lend you money out of what we have to use from other people's deposits. You will pay a certain 'interest' upon it (that is, so much a year on each hundred pounds we lend you – say £5 a year for every £100), and you shall pay us back when you can." The bank accompanied this offer with the right to draw further cheques to, say, another thousand pounds, which the bank would "honour" – that is, for which the bank would pay out money which did not really belong to their client but was lent to him by the bank out of other people's balances. And this extra amount, which the bank thus allowed their client over and beyond what was his own money was, and is, called an "overdraft."

At first, before the banks would allow anybody an "overdraft" (that is, a loan), they required the borrower to give security. He had to leave with them gold or silver plate or a mortgage upon his land, so that if, in the long run, he found himself unable to pay back, the banker could sell the security and recoup himself.

But it was obviously convenient and useful when a client was in a big way of business to grant him an "overdraft" from time to time although he had no security to offer. The bank said to itself: "Here is a merchant making very large profits every year. It takes him some time to get his money in from the foreigners to whom he sells goods overseas, but he is bound to get it sooner or later. So, without asking him for any security (for perhaps he has no plate or title deeds or what not to give), it is still well worth our while to let him have an overdraft (that is, a loan) out of the other people's money. He will pay us interest upon it, we shall make a profit, and when the foreigners pay him he will be able to pay us back."

In this way the banks became on all sides lenders of money to persons without security, and it became exceedingly important to any trader whether he could or could not get the banks to back him up in this fashion.

The thing went farther. A man might have no capital at all, but a good idea. He might have discovered, for instance, a mine of copper-ore in some colony. He would come to the banks and say: "I have not the money to pay labourers to dig for this ore, but if you will advance the money to me and go shares in the profit the ore can be got out." The banks would look at the "proposition," as it is called, and if they thought it a good thing they would advance the money and share the subsequent profits with the borrower. All over the world the banks were thus "financing," as it is called, every kind of enterprise.

The system went farther still – and here it is that we come upon the modern trouble. Hitherto when they gave an overdraft to anybody, whether with or without security, or even when they gave a loan to a man who had no capital at all, and "backed" him in his enterprise which they thought likely to prove successful, they had used the money which other clients had left with them. But it occurred to the banks after a certain time that there was no need to use anybody else's money at all. *They could themselves offer to honour the cheques of the man to whom they lent the money without having any real money with which to pay those cheques.*

Why was this? It was because, with the growth of the Banking System, hardly any of the payments were, by this time, actually made in gold. Real money only passed in a very small degree. Of the myriad transactions all but a tiny proportion were "instruments of credit." Just as a bank-note issued by the Bank of England is a promise to pay in gold, and yet a promise to pay a million pounds in bank-notes could always be made with much less than a million real pounds to redeem the notes, so *the banks could create paper money, or its equivalent, in the form of overdrafts.* If they said to a man who had *no* money deposited with them: "We will honour your cheques up to £1,000," *what they were really doing was increasing the paper currency to the extent of £1,000.* They were issuing promises to pay, exactly like bank-notes, knowing that of the total amount out only a small proportion at any moment would be required in real money.

There was a check on this system of creating new artificial paper money by the banks (for this is what it came to), and the check

consisted in the control of the Government over the National Bank
– in England the Bank of England. There was a law preventing the
Bank of England from issuing more than a certain number of notes
in proportion to the gold lying behind them, and the private banks
could not issue overdrafts, or loans, indefinitely, because they could
not get more than a certain amount of paper money from the Bank
of England to meet the payments they had to make, and the Bank,
in its turn, could not issue more than a certain proportion of paper
money against its gold.

So ultimately the amount of real money, the gold, in the hands
of the banks, both national and private, acted as a check upon this
creation of false money by the banks. But when gold payments
ceased with the Great War that check broke down, and even if gold
payments had not ceased, the power of the banks thus to "create"
as it is called – in other words, their power to say to any individual
enterprise: "You shall or you shall not have your cheques honoured:
you shall or you shall not carry on" – gave them an immense and
increasing power over the community.

That is why the revolt against the Banking System and its
control over our lives in the modern state since the war is becoming
so formidable.

It has two chief forms against which men protest.

1. The bankers can decide, of two competitors, which shall
survive. As the great majority of enterprises lie in debt to the banks
– that is, carrying on with loans allowed them by the banks working
with money *made* by the banks – any one of two competing indus-
tries can be killed by the bankers saying: "I will no longer lend you
this money. I 'call it in' – that is, ask for it to be paid at once. But I
will not exercise the same pressure upon the man who is competing
against you." This power makes the banks the masters of the greater
part of modern industry. It is argued that the banks do not act from
caprice, and will naturally only back a sound enterprise and only ruin
an unsound one. That is, on the whole, true. But still, those who
command them have the power, if they like, to act from caprice, and
whenever you give a few human beings great power of this sort over
millions of others it tends to be abused.

2. The banks, especially in England, are all in one combination and keep detailed information upon all of us. Not only have they control over industry through their power to make or withhold the money which they alone can now create and hand out to those they favour, but they also keep indexes of detailed information as thorough and widespread as those of any Government office. They have a secret service more widespread and powerful than that of the State, and this hidden power of theirs, though private and concealed knowledge, irritates plain men more and more. People feel that they are not free, and that the Banking System, which is international in essence, is a universal and hidden master.

Therefore all over the world today people are saying: "The Banking System, and the few men who direct it, are altogether too powerful. They control our lives. They are beginning to control the public policy of the State, especially in England, and there ought to be a national authority superior to them and keeping them in order."

A great many schemes have lately been on all sides proposed to establish a superior authority. Thus, we have in England a very powerful movement in favour of what is called the "Douglas Scheme of Credit," and of course the Socialists, with their ideas of State control of everything, would also put an end to the private power of the Banking System. Then there are those who want to have a strong King who would be able to override any lesser power in the State, including the bankers.† But the points to seize in understanding the political economy of our time are those I have just been describing to you: what the Banking System is, how it arose, how unnaturally powerful it has become, and why a universal revolt is arising against it.

There will be a struggle inevitably between the banking, or financial, interest and the people all over civilised countries: but no one can tell which will win. In industrial countries the odds are in favour of the banks, or financiers. In peasant countries against them.

---

† In theory Parliament is stronger than the banks, but Parliament no longer counts as a real governing power. The banks are far more powerful than Parliament.

IX

NATIONAL LOANS AND TAXATION

EVERY country must, to carry on its national services, raise taxes from its citizens, and those taxes, though levied in money, translate themselves, of course, into goods, that is, economic values attached to material objects.

We say that the State "raises," say, a hundred million pounds in taxation from its citizens a year, for "State Purposes"; and when you come to look into what is actually got by the State and how the State uses what it has got, it means that the State levies so many boots and so much bread, and so much housing material and so much clothing, and spends this again in maintaining State servants, that is, in clothing and housing and feeding soldiers and policemen, and civil servants and school teachers and so on.

But in the modern world, and for the last two hundred years or so, nearly all states have also had to raise taxation *in order to pay interest upon the State loans.*

A State loan, or NATIONAL DEBT, arises in this way. The State needs a great quantity of goods for a particular purpose – usually for the very unproductive purpose of waging a war. It has to get a lot of metal for its munitions and guns, and quantities of food to feed the soldiers, and coal to transport them. Now there are two ways in which a state gets these. The first is to get the whole amount, as it is needed, directly from the people, by a very heavy tax levied at the time. That was what was done for hundreds of years before the second method was attempted. The king of a country, wishing to wage war, would ask his subjects for contributions, and he could not wage war upon a scale more than these contributions would meet.

But about two hundred years ago there began (and since then has very largely increased), the second method, which is that of NATIONAL LOANS.

The State is, let us say, taking in ordinary taxation from its citizens about one-tenth of their produce. Suddenly it finds itself involved in a much higher expenditure, amounting to, say, half the produce of the country. If it asked for half the produce right away as a tax people might refuse to pay it, or it might make the policy of the State – the war, for instance, which the Government wanted to wage – so unpopular that the State could not pursue that policy or wage that war. So the Government had recourse to *borrowing* from the citizens, promising to pay, to those who lent, interest in proportion to what they borrowed, as well as the capital itself. Thus they would *take* in taxation for a war money from a farmer equivalent to *ten* loads of wheat; but they would also *borrow* from him *one hundred loads* of wheat, promising to give him as interest *five* loads of wheat every year for any number of years until they should ultimately pay back the whole hundred loads as well.

When these national loans began the Governments honestly intended to pay back what they borrowed. But the method was so fatally easy that, as time went on, the debt piled up and up until there could be no question of repaying it: all the State could do was to pay the interest out of taxation. It remained indebted to private rich men for the principal, that is, the whole original sum, and meanwhile, through further wars, this hold of the rich men upon all the rest of the community perpetually increased.

The "National Debt" – as it came to be called – remained a permanent institution, in connection with which all the citizens had to be taxed in order to provide interest for the rich lenders. Latterly these burdens of national debt have become overwhelming, and at the present moment about a twelfth of everything that English people produce is taken from them and handed over as interest to the comparatively few wealthy residents in England and abroad who lent great sums to the Government during the war.

It is true that whenever a loan is raised the Government provides not only interest but what is called a "sinking fund" – that is, an extra amount of taxation every year which is dedicated to paying back the whole of the loan slowly. But long before a loan is paid off some new occasion rises compelling the Government to borrow again on a large scale, and the total debt perpetually increases.

The result is that all the great modern European nations are now loaded with a debt really larger than any of them can bear, and that therefore they have all taken steps to lighten that burden by various tricks not at all straightforward. Some of them pay back in money which appears the same as the money which they borrowed, but which has a very different value. They have borrowed for a war, say, £1,000, representing 100 tons of wheat. Then they debase the currency, so that a sum still called £1,000 will only buy 20 tons of wheat, and in this way they can pretend to pay the lender back, although they are really cheating him of four-fifths of what he lent. Two countries, Germany and Russia, have pushed this so far that the lenders are now not really paid anything at all. A man who lent the German Government, for carrying on the war, money which during the war would have bought a million tons of wheat, is now (October, 1923) paid back in money called by the same name but able only to purchase a tenth of a ton – which is the same as saying that he is not paid back at all.

Of all European countries that fought in the war our own has been the most honest in this matter, but even in England a man who lent the equivalent of 1,000 sheep, say, and who was promised interest at the rate of 50 sheep a year, is only getting 25 sheep a year on account of the change in the value of money.

In this matter of loans we must distinguish between "internal loans" and "external loans." An internal loan is borrowed from one's own people. It involves taxing and impoverishing one set of citizens in order to pay interest to and enrich another set. But the country as a whole is no poorer. An external loan is borrowed from foreigners, and the interest on it is dead loss to the country. Also, it cannot be paid in debased currency. A government can cheat its own nationals by paying them in false money. But it has to pay foreign lenders in real money. A foreign loan is real. It must be (as a rule) paid in gold. England thus pays millions a year to America.

Now from State *loans* let us turn to State *taxation,* which has today for its most permanent object the payment of interest on internal and external loans.

How does the State tax its citizens?

Taxation levied by the State is divided into two kinds – called "direct" and "indirect."

Direct taxation is the taxation levied upon the money which the person who pays it has at his disposal.

For instance: If you have £1,000 a year and the State makes you declare that and then taxes you £100 every year, that is direct taxation.

Indirect taxation takes the form of levying a tax on the manufacturer of an article or on the importer of an article, which tax he passes on to the person who consumes it, by an addition to the price of the article. Thus, when you buy a pound of tea or a bottle of wine you are paying indirect taxation. The price which you paid for the tea is so much for the real value of the tea and so much more (though you do not feel or know it at the time) which has been paid on the tea as it came into England at the ports. The brewers who make beer have got to pay the Government so much for every gallon they make, and this is passed on to the people who buy the beer by an extra amount put on to the price.

The wisest men who have discussed how taxes should be levied laid down four rules which, unfortunately, no Government has kept to as it should. It is worth while knowing those rules, because they are a guide to what good taxation should be.

These rules are:—

1. A tax should fall in such a fashion that it is paid most easily.

For instance: it is much easier to pay £100 a year in small sums which fall due at frequent intervals than to pay the whole £100 upon demand in one lump.

2. The tax should be so arranged that the cost of collecting it should be as slight as possible.

For instance: If I put a tax upon everyone who crosses a particular bridge, I shall have to appoint and pay someone to collect the tax at the bridge, and I shall probably have to pay inspectors to go round and see that these bridgemen do their duty and do not cheat. If I tried to levy a tax of this kind on a great many bridges that are not much used the cost of collecting would be very high compared with the revenue produced. But if I put a tax on every cheque issued by a bank, *that* tax is collected with hardly any expense. All the Government has to do is to say that no cheque will be valid unless it carries a stamp. The banks stamp all their cheques with this stamp, and when they sell a cheque book to a customer they take the value of the stamps from him. All the Government has to do is to find out the number of cheque books issued, and ask for the money from the banks.†

3. Taxes are better in proportion as they fall on unnecessary things rather than on necessary things.

It is much better, obviously, to make people pay for their luxuries than for their necessities. It is oppressive to make people pay for their necessities, which even the very poor must have, and it is juster and altogether better to make people pay for things which they need not have. Thus, when the tax was first levied upon tea it was a tax upon a luxury, for only rich people then drank tea. But today, when the poorest people must drink it, it is unjust to tax it, for it is a necessity.

Unfortunately, it is very difficult to keep to this rule in any modern country, because the amount of taxes required is so large that unless one taxes the necessities one will not get enough money for the requirements of the State: thus tea and sugar, beer and tobacco, all of them *necessities* of the poorest people, are enormously taxed. Our poor people in England are much more heavily taxed than any people in the world.

4. Taxes should fall proportionately to the wealth of the taxed, that is, the sacrifice should be equally felt by all. This rule is easy enough to keep when taxation is light. For a very slight tax on poor men – who are the vast majority of the State, suffices to bring in the small revenue needed, and a severe tax on rich men is but an addition. But when taxation must be heavy to meet the requirements of the State – say more than a twentieth of poor men's incomes – then the rule is difficult to keep. For either you get insufficient revenue if you spare the poor, or you must tax the poor on a scale which no increase of the taxation on the rich can really equal. When taxation is too heavy, you must either ruin the rich or crush the poor. And that is why heavy taxation has destroyed so many States.

5. The last rule about taxation is that it should be *certain;* and this means that the State should be certain of getting what it ought to get, and that the people who pay should know what they have to pay and not be left in doubt and anxiety.

---

† This very sensible tax was invented by Disraeli in England about a lifetime ago.

For instance: the tax on tobacco in this country is a certain tax. It is levied on a comparatively small number of ships' cargoes which enter the country with tobacco, because we do not grow tobacco in England, and the sum which the importers pay is automatically passed on to the purchasers. The State knows by experience how much tobacco the people will buy in the country in the year, and the people who buy tobacco know what they mean to spend, and can, if they choose, ascertain how much of this goes in taxation. But the same tax on tobacco in France is not a certain tax, because the French grow a lot of their own tobacco – in fact, most of it. The people who grow tobacco naturally try to hide the total amount of their crop from the Government inspectors, and a great number of these inspectors have to be going about the whole time actually counting each leaf on each plant and rummaging in the bins to see that none is gone.

An example of a most uncertain and unjust tax for the taxpayer in our own country is the Income Tax, because it is difficult to prevent unfixed people from hiding their profits or from concealing from the tax collectors amounts which they have earned. Also the honest citizen with an established and known position can be bled to the full, while the rogue and the adventurer, the speculator and dealer escapes. But it is a certain tax from the point of view of the Government, because they know on the average what a penny on the Income Tax will produce one year with another, and are not concerned with justice but with a calculable revenue.

Before we leave this discussion it is worth while mentioning an odd idea which a few very earnest and active people have got hold of, called the "Single Tax."

It is really much more a part of the theory of Socialism than a system of taxation. Still, as it has come to be called the "Single Tax" we will treat it under that head.

The idea of the single tax is this:— Rent, or the surplus value of a site, whether it be due to the extra fertility of farm land or to the extra convenience of town land, is, say the Single Taxers, not the product of the individual who owns the land.

If I own a barren piece of heath on which I cannot get any rent for agriculture, and then a railway is built passing through it and a station is built on the heath, many town workers who want to live in the country will take houses which will be built near this station and live in these houses, running up and down from town for their work. In a few years this barren heath which brought me in nothing will be bringing in many thousands a year, for a little town will have sprang up, and I shall be able to charge rent to all the people who live there upon my land.

The Single Taxers say that, since I did nothing towards making the extra value, but that extra value has been made by the growth of population and by the activity of the whole community, I have no right to these rents. In the same way they say that I have no right to the rent of a very fertile field compared with a bad field which pays little or no rent, because it was not I that made the soil fertile.

So they propose that *all the rents of the country should be levied as a tax*. They say that no other taxes are needed. If I have money from dividends in an industrial concern I can keep all that without paying any taxes on it, and I can be let off taxes on tobacco and drink and everything else of that sort. But anything I get as rent for land I must pay over to the State. I may still be allowed to call myself the owner of the land, but I must be taxed an equivalent to the rent which it produces.

These people have never been able to apply their theory, and the reason is pretty clear. It would work most unjustly, considering that people buy and sell land just as they do any other commodity, and that a man who had put all his money into rents in land would be ruined by this system, while another man with exactly the same amount of money, who had put it into a business, would go scot free. If you were starting a new country it might be possible to begin with the Single Tax system, but even then you would be up against the fact that people like owning land because such ownership gives them independence. But at any rate it is theoretically possible to apply this system in a new country. In an old country it is quite out of the question.

X

THE SOCIAL (OR HISTORICAL) VALUE
OF MONEY

THERE is a special point in Economics which has been very little dealt with, or rather not properly dealt with at all, and which you will find interesting as a new piece of study, because it will help you to understand history as nothing else will: and that point is the SOCIAL (OR HISTORICAL) VALUE OF MONEY.

You read how, in the past, the King of England, wishing to wage a great war, managed to raise, say, a hundred thousand pounds; and how that was thought a most enormous sum: whereas today, for the same sized army, we should need thirty times as much. You read how Henry VIII suppressed the Monastery at Westminster which had an income of four thousand pounds a year, and how this income was then regarded as something very large indeed – much as we today regard a half million a year or more – the income of some great shipping company. You read how the National Debt later on actually reached *one* million, and people trembled lest the State could not bear the burden.

Yet here we are today, raising hundreds of millions yearly in taxation, spending thousands of millions in our wars.

What is the explanation of this apparently totally different meaning of money in different times? It puzzles nearly everybody who reads history intelligently, and it wants explanation. Most attempts to explain it have failed, or have been very insufficient; some of them quite vague, as: "The value of money was very different in those days from what it is now." Or: "Money was then at least ten times as valuable as now" (whereas it is clear from the chronicle that it was *enormously* more valuable!). Sentences like that leave the unfortunate reader as much in the dark as he was before. We need a more precise explanation, and that I think can be given.

There are three things which, between them, decide the social value of money at any period, and unless we consider *all* three we shall go wrong. The reason why most people have gone wrong in trying to solve the problem – or have abandoned it – is that they only consider the first of the three. These three things are as follows:—

1. *The actual purchasing power of whatever is used as currency* – in our case, for nearly the whole of European history, gold:† the amount of wheat and leather and building materials and all the rest of it, which so much weight of gold (say an ounce) will purchase at any time. This varies in different periods according to the amount of gold present in circulation, and its efficiency in circulation. We saw how these were the factors of price, that is, of the purchasing power of money, when we spoke of money earlier in the book.

2. *The number of kinds of things* which money can be used to buy in any society – or, to put it in learned words, "the number of categories of purchasable economic values."

3. *The economic scale of the community,* that is, the number of its citizens and the amount of its total wealth at a given time.

When we go into the full meaning of all these three things we shall see how, in combination, they make up the social value of money at any time, and why that value differs so very much between one historical period and another.

1. The Actual Purchasing Power of the Currency

Given the same currency (and in Western Europe it has, for all practical purposes, been gold for the last two thousand years), we can measure the purchasing value of such and such a weight of gold in any period by what is known as the "Index Number" of that period.

The Index Number is a thing important to understand, because it comes into a great deal of modern discussion as well as historical discussion; for instance: wages are nowadays largely based upon an Index Number.

A particular year is taken, say the year 1900, and the records of what various commodities were fetching in gold in the market during that year are examined. Thus it is found that an ounce of gold in that

---

† Silver and gold were used together, but gold alone will serve as a test.

year would buy (let us say) four hundred pounds weight of wheat, 600 pounds weight of barley, 80 pounds weight of bacon, 80 gallons of beer, a quarter of a ton of pig iron, and so on. A list is drawn up of all the principal commodities which are used in the community. Suppose that 100 such commodities are taken and between them make up by far the great part – say seven-eighths – of all the values commonly consumed in that community. The next thing to do is what is called to "weight" each commodity, for it is evident that a commodity which is very largely bought – such as bread – must count more in estimating the purchasing power of money than a commodity of which very much less is used – such as tin.

According to the value of each commodity used in any one period of time (say a year) the various commodities are "weighted." Thus you count bread (let us say) as twelve times more important than lead, because the value of the bread used in the community for one year is twelve times as much as the value of the lead used in the community during that year. Then let us suppose that the value of the leather used is three times that of the lead, the value of the iron five times, etc. You put against each commodity these "weight" numbers.

Next you find out what an ounce of gold would purchase of each of those commodities in that particular year. For instance: you find it would purchase a quarter of a ton of lead, 400 pounds weight of bread, and so on, only you multiply by your weight number the use of gold in each particular article. For instance: you count the gold used in buying bread as twelve times more important than the gold used in buying lead.

You then add up all the prices measured in an ounce of gold in your column; you divide by the number of items in your column, each multiplied by its weight number, and the result is that your ounce of gold for the year 1900 will be found to have a certain *average purchasing power* which you call, for the sake of further application, arbitrarily, "100."

Then you take another year, say 1920, and you find what the ounce of gold would purchase in the same conditions, similarly weighted, in the year 1920. You discover that the ounce of gold on the average in 1920 would only purchase half the weight of stuff it purchased in 1900. In other words, prices have doubled, or, what is the same thing, gold has halved in value. You put down for the year 1920 the figure "200," which means that average prices are twice as great as they were in 1900, and the economist's way of saying this is: "With the year 1900 as a base, the Index Number for 1920 is 200."

In the year 1921 he makes the calculation again, and finds that prices have fallen, that is, gold has become rather more valuable as compared with other things, and prices are only three-quarters more than they were in 1900. The economist writes down: "The Index Number for 1921 is 175, with the prices of 1900 as a base." He goes back to 1880 and finds that in 1880, after making a similar calculation, an ounce of gold would on the average buy five pounds of material where in 1900 it could only buy four. In other words, prices are lower in 1880 by one-fourth. So he writes down: "The Index Number for 1880, with 1900 as a base, is 75."

These Index Numbers taken for each year with a particular year as a "base," or year of reference, show the fluctuations in the purchasing value of gold.

To make the process clearer, we will take a simple instance and imagine a community in which there were only three things purchased on a large scale by the citizens – wheat, bacon, and iron. We take for our year of reference, let us say, the year 1880, and we find that an ounce of gold would purchase one ton of wheat, half a ton of iron, and a quarter of a ton of bacon. But the amount spent on wheat was ten times the amount spent on bacon and twenty times the amount spent on iron.

You add up the twenty tons of wheat, the half ton of iron and the half ton of bacon – half a ton of the latter because twice as much is spent on it as is spent on iron, and therefore though it is half the price of iron you must double the amount, because twice as much is bought.

You get 21 tons. To buy this 21 tons of stuff 3 ounces of gold were needed. You divide the 21 tons by 3, and you get 7 tons of material on the average.

Next, as you are taking this particular year for a "base" (or year of reference) you call the 7 "100," so that you may compare in percentages the rise or fall of prices in other years. You then do exactly the same thing with these three staple commodities in another year – say 1890 – and you find that your ounce of gold purchases no longer 7 tons of stuff, but 14 tons of stuff. Taking the year 1880 as your base number, you will see that the Index Number for 1890 is "50."

Then you do the same thing for the year 1920, and you find that with the same ounce of gold you can only purchase 3½ tons of stuff. 7 is to 3½ as 100 is to 200, so the Index Number for 1920 will be 200 as compared with the base year – or year of reference – which is 1880.

You cannot use the Index Numbers without knowing what your base year is and what average prices were in that base year, but, having settled that, your Index Number is nothing more than a statement of *average prices,* or again, the average purchasing power of a fixed weight of gold in the various epochs you examine.

In reality the calculating of an Index Number involves a great many more difficult points than these, and of course the number of commodities taken is very much more than three; but that is the method in its general outline, and if you go over it carefully I think you will not find it difficult to understand.†

The first thing, then, in finding out the social value of money at any historical period is to find out the purchasing value of a given weight of gold – say, one ounce. Supposing we are comparing the time when Henry VIII dissolved the monasteries and took their wealth (1536–9) with our own time, before the War, when our currency was still normal and in gold, you will find that with 100 as your base for prices in 1536–9 the Index Number of 1913 is, according to different calculations, somewhere between 2,000 and 2,400. I have gone into it myself very carefully, and I make it out to be at least 2,400 (though historians some time ago, who had not gone into it very fully, used to make it lower); that is, where one ounce of gold would purchase the things which Englishmen regarded as their staple commodities in 1536, 24 ounces of gold would be necessary today.

That is the first thing you have to consider when you are comparing the social value of money at that time with the social value of money in our own time. You multiply right away by 24. You hear, for instance, that a man had £100 a year paid him by the King

---

† A simple daily example of an amateur index number is the housewife's idea of "cost of living." She finds that, for the purchase of her home, a great deal of bread, a little butter, more cheese, so much for clothing, rent, etc., 40s. today go about as far as 20s. in 1913 before the war. In other words she is "taking 1913 as a base and establishing an index number of 200 for 1923."

for looking after the garrison at Dover. You translate it into modern money, and say that he had £2,400 a year paid him "in our money."

Most people stop there, and that is why they get their answer to the problem all wrong. In reality the *social* value of money then was *very much more* than 24 times what it is now, and £100 a year under Henry VIII meant *a great deal more than* what £2,400 means now.

In order to see how true this is we have to consider the next two points which I mentioned.

2. The Number of Purchasable Categories

Suppose you put a man into a little primitive place like Andorra (which is a tiny independent state shut off from the world in a valley of the Pyrenees), and he is paid there £1,000 a year. He cannot live in a house with more than a small rental, because there are no big houses to be had. Everybody lives in simple, little houses. He cannot spend his money on many things. There are no roads, no use for a motor car; no railways, so he cannot spend money on railway fares; no theatres or cinematographs – none of the hundred things which we have here on every side. He can buy bread and meat, and wine and clothing, and very little else – for there is nothing else to be bought. In other words, the number of *sets of things* (that is what the word "categories" means – "sets of things") on which he can spend money is a great deal less than what it would be in London. A man with £1,000 a year in London and a family to keep is, of course, very much better off than a labouring man, but still he is not rich, as rich people use the term. He will live in a house for which he must pay perhaps £200 a year, counting rent and taxes. Then he will – he usually must – travel, and that will cost him perhaps £50 a year. Then his friends will expect to meet him and he must have them at his house, and he will have to spend a good deal in postage and telegraphing – and so on. The man in Andorra with £1,000 a year simply would not know what to do with it. He would be so "well off" that he would have a very large surplus – more than half – to give away, or to help other people with, or to save and invest. But exactly the same sort of man, with the same ideas and bringing-up and necessities, put down in London would certainly not be able to save a penny of his £1,000 a year.

So we see that the social value of £1,000 a year in Andorra is very different from the social value of the same sum in London. Some people might be inclined to laugh at this difference, and to say: "Oh, yes! but the man in London could, if he liked, save, simply by not spending on those various categories, as you call them." Yes; he as an individual might choose to live an odd life of his own and not do what other people do. But *Society as a whole* – that is, all the community round him – in London is, as a fact, spending upon those various, very numerous, categories, while in Andorra he does not, for he *cannot*, spend upon them; they are not there to be purchased. Therefore it is true that the *social value* of the same sum, with the same index number, is on the average very much higher in Andorra than in London.

You cannot give this difference precisely in figures as you can an index number, because nobody can precisely calculate the number of categories nor the respective importance of each, but the least knowledge of history shows you that in Henry VIII's time, in 1536, the number of categories was very much smaller than it is today. So the man to whom Henry VIII paid £100 a year as salary for looking after one of his castles, though the purchasing value of his income – the amount of rye or pork or what not that he could buy with it – was what we should call today £2,400 a year, had a much higher income *relatively to the people of the time* than has a man with £2,400 a year today. He counted much more than a man today counts who has five thousand a year.

But this second point is not all. There is again a third point, as we have seen, and we must next turn to that.

3. The Purchasing Value of the Whole Community

The third factor in the making up of the social value of money is the relation of any sum to the total wealth of the whole community. That of course depends upon two things: the average of wealth of each family in the community, and the number of those families.

Supposing, for instance, with things at their present prices, you consider two communities: (1) the people of Iceland, (2) the people of Australia. In both countries you can get pretty much the same

amount of stuff for an ounce of gold, and though there are less categories of purchasable things in Iceland than in Australia, yet most
of the things a civilised man requires can be got in Iceland – at least
in the capital, or can be imported there by the inhabitants if they need
them or can afford to pay for them. Both communities are of our own
race and of much the same standard of culture and the same idea of
how one should live. But Iceland has only four thousand families,
and these families are poor for the most part. Australia has a million
families, that is, 250 times as many, and they are much richer than
the families in Iceland on the average. There are much worse differences of rich and poor in Australia than there are in Iceland. There
are far more miserable and starving people in Australia than there
are in Iceland; but the *average* wealth of a family in Australia is much
higher than that in Iceland.

Now suppose that the Government of Iceland were to want to
build a new harbour for the capital, which is on the sea, and in order
to get the money were either to confiscate the wealth of certain rich
people or to tax all the people – supposing it wanted, for instance,
£400,000 in order to complete the work. And supposing the people
of Australia similarly wanted to build a harbour and also wanted
£400,000 to be got in the same way. The index number is the same
in both places. An ounce of gold will roughly purchase the same
amount of things in both places, for the index number at any moment
is much the same all over the white world, measured in gold, and we
may imagine the categories of purchasable things to be much the
same in both places. Yet the social value of the £400,000 is quite
different in Iceland from what it is in Australia. In Iceland it means
taking an average of £100 from each of the poor families – if you
get it by taxation – or the confiscation of all the wealth of the very
few rich men there may be. But in Australia it means no more than
the taking of about 8s. from each family, and that from an average family income much higher than the average family income in
Iceland. Under this heading the social value of £400,000 in Iceland
is enormous and in Australia is small. If Iceland tried to build such
a harbour it could hardly do so. The economic effort would be very
great, and if it succeeded it would fill a big place in the history of the
island. In Australian history it would pass almost unnoticed.

Now let us add the influence of all these three points together,
and we shall see that there is a vast difference between the social

value of money in the time of Henry VIII, when the monasteries were dissolved, and the social value of the same amount of money today. We shall see, for instance, why the King, taking away the annual revenues of the Monastery of Westminster and keeping them for himself, made such a prodigious splash, although the actual amount in pounds, or weight of gold, in which the income of Westminster Abbey could then be measured was only £4,000 a year. In the first place, you must multiply by 24, so that the actual income or annual purchasing value in wheat, beef, rye, pork, beer, which was confiscated, was nearly £100,000 in our money. Then you must remember that it took place in a community where there was a very much smaller number of purchasable categories; that is, where people had a very much smaller number of "sets of things" upon which to spend money.

And, lastly, you must remember that it took place in an England the population of which was hardly more than a sixth – some people would say it was hardly more than a tenth – of today's, and that population actually a great deal poorer on the average than the present population of England. It is true that there was not then the great herd of starving or half-starving people which we have today in England, and that labouring people were then much better off than they are now; but, on the other hand, there was nothing like the same number of very rich people, and therefore the average family income was much smaller. Put all that together, and it is clear what a tremendous business the confiscation of this one Abbey meant. It was somewhat as though the Government today were to confiscate one of the smaller railway companies, or to take away the rentals now paid by a northern manufacturing town to the great landlords owning the soil, and put the money into its own pocket.

From this example of the confiscation of the Abbey of Westminster you can argue to all the other expenditure of the time – expenditure on armies and navies, and so on – and in this way you can see *how, why and in what degree the social value of money differs between one period and another.*

It is most important to get this point in Economics clear in your mind if you are reading history, because it helps to explain all manner of things which otherwise puzzle one in the past.

XI

USURY

USURY, the last subject but one on which I am going to touch in this book, is one which modern people have almost entirely forgotten, and which you will not find mentioned in any book on Economics that I know. Yet its vital importance was recognised throughout all history until quite lately, and it is already forcing itself upon modern people's notice whether they like it or no. So it is as well to understand it betimes, for it is going to be discussed very widely in the near future.

All codes of law and all writers on morals from the beginning of anything we know about human society have denounced as wrong the practice of USURY.

They have recognised that this practice does grave harm to the State and to society as a whole, and must, therefore, as far as possible, be forbidden.

Now what is Usury, and why does it thus do harm?

Modern people have so far forgotten this exceedingly important matter that they have come to use the word "usury" loosely for "the taking of high interest upon a loan." That is very muddled thinking indeed, as you will see in a moment. The character of Usury *has nothing to do with the taking of high or low interest.* It is concerned with something quite different.

Usury is the taking of any interest whatever upon an UNPRODUC-TIVE *loan.*

A man comes to you and says: "Lend me this piece of capital which you possess" (for instance, a ship, and stores of food with which to feed the sailors during the voyage of the ship). "Using this piece of capital to transport the surplus goods from this country over the sea and to bring back foreign goods which we need here I shall make a profit so large that I can exchange it for at least one hundred tons of wheat. The voyage there and back will take a year."

You naturally answer: "It is all very well for you to make a profit of one hundred tons of wheat in one year by the use of *my* ship and of *my* stores of food for sailors who work the ship, but what about me? I grant you ought to have part of this profit for yourself, as you are taking all the trouble. But I ought to have *some,* because the ship and stores of food are mine; and unless I lent them to you (since you have none of your own) you would not be able to make that profit by trading of which you speak. Let us go half shares. You shall have fifty tons of wheat and I will take fifty, out of the total profit of one hundred tons."

The man who proposed to borrow your ship agrees. The bargain is struck, and when the year is over you make a fifty tons profit of wheat on your capital.

That is *the earning of interest on a productive loan.*

There is nothing morally wrong about that transaction at all. It does no one any harm. It does not weaken the State or society, or even hurt any individual. There is a sheer gain due to wise exchange (which is equivalent to production); everybody is benefited – you that own the capital, the man who uses it, and all society, which benefits by the foreign exchange. Supposing your ship and stores of food were worth a hundred tons of wheat, then your profit of fifty tons of wheat is a profit of fifty percent, which is very high indeed. But you have a perfect right to it: your capital has produced a real increase of wealth to that extent. If your capital be worth ten times as much, then your profit is only five percent instead of fifty. But your moral right to the fifty percent is just as great as your moral right to the five percent. No one can blame you, and you are doing no harm.

Now supposing that, instead of coming to ask you for the loan of your ship, the man came and asked you for the loan of a sum of money which you happened to have by you and which would be sufficient to buy and stock the ship. It is clear that the transaction remains exactly the same. The loan is *productive.* He makes a true profit, that is, there is a real increase of wealth for the community, and you and he have a right to take your shares out of it – you because you are the owner of the capital, and he because he took the trouble of organising and overlooking the expedition.

These are examples of profit on a *productive* loan.

Now suppose a man to come to you if you were a baker and say: "Lend me half a dozen loaves. My family have no bread and I cannot see my way to earning anything for a day or two. But when I begin to earn I will get another half dozen loaves and see that you are not out of pocket." Then if you were to reply: "I will not let you have half a dozen loaves on those terms. I will let you owe me the bread for a month if you like, but at the end of the month you must give me back *seven* loaves": that would be usury.

The man is not using the loan productively; he is consuming the loaves immediately. No more wealth is created by the act. The world is not the richer, nor are you the richer, nor is society in general the richer. No more wealth at all has appeared through the transaction. Therefore the extra loaf that you are claiming is claimed out of nothing. It has to come out of the wealth of the community – in this particular case out of the wealth of the man who borrowed the loaves – instead of coming out of an increment or excess or new wealth. That is why Usury is called "Usury" – which means: "wearing down," "gradually dilapidating."

It is clear that if the whole world practised usury and nothing but usury, if wealth were never lent to be used productively, but only to be consumed unproductively, and yet were to demand interest on the unproductive transaction, then the wealth that was lent would soon eat up all the other wealth in the community until you came to a situation in which there was no more to take. Everyone would be ruined except those who lent; then these, having no more blood to suck, would die themselves, and society would end.

As in the case of the ship, it matters not in the least whether the actual thing, the loaves of bread, are lent, or money is lent with which to buy them. *The test is whether the loan is productive or not.* The *intention* of Usury is present *when the money is lent at interest on what the lender* KNOWS *will be an unproductive purpose,* and the actual *practice* of Usury is present *when the loan, having as a fact been used unproductively, interest is none the less demanded.*

As in every other case of right and wrong whatsoever, there is, of course, a broad margin in which it is very difficult to draw the line. A man guilty of usury and trying to excuse himself might say, even in the case of food lent to a starving man: "The loan may not look directly productive, but indirectly it *was* productive, for it saved the man's life and thus later on he was able to work and produce wealth."

The other way about (though there is not much danger of that nowadays), a man trying to get out of interest on a productive loan might say in many cases: "The loan was not really productive. It is true I made a profit on it, but that profit was not additional wealth for the community. It only represented what I got out of somebody else on a bargain."

In this margin of uncertainty we have only common sense to guide us, as in every other similar case. We know pretty well in each particular example we come across whether a loan is productive or not; whether we are borrowing or lending for a productive purpose, or for a charitable or luxurious one, or for one in every way unproductive.

The proof that this feeling about usury is right is to be found in the private conduct of individuals in their social relations. If a poor man in distress goes to a rich friend and borrows ten pounds, he pays it back when he can; and the rich man would think it dishonourable to charge interest. But if a man borrowed ten pounds of one for the purpose of doing something which was likely to increase its value, and we knew that this was his purpose, we should have a perfect right to share the results with him, and no one would think the claim dishonourable.

Usury, then, is essentially a claim to increment, or extra wealth, *which is not there to be claimed.* It is a practice which diminishes the capital wealth of the needy and eats it up to the profit of the lender; so that, if Usury go unchecked, it must end in the absorption of all private property into the hands of a few money brokers.

Now, these things being so, the nature of Usury being pretty clear, and both the moral wrong of it and the injury it does to society being equally clear, how is it that the modern world for so long forgot all about it, and how is it that it is forcing itself upon the attention of the modern world again in spite of that forgetfulness?

I will answer both of those questions.

The wrong and the very nature of Usury came to be forgotten with the great expansion of financial dealings which arose in the middle and end of the seventeenth century – that is, about 250 years ago – in Europe. In the simpler times, when commercial transactions were open and upon a comparatively small scale, and done between men who knew each other, you could pretty usually tell, as you can in private life, whether a loan were a loan required for a productive or an unproductive purpose. The burden of proof lay upon the lender. It was no excuse in lending a man money to say: "I did not know what he wanted to do with it, so I charged him 10 percent, thinking that very probably he was going to use it productively." The courts of justice would not admit such a plea, and they were quite right. For under the simple conditions of the old days the judge would answer: "It was your business to know. A man does not come borrowing money unless he is in either personal necessity or has some productive scheme for which he wants to use the money. If you thought it was a productive scheme you would certainly have asked him about it in order to share the profits, and the fact that you did not trouble to find out whether it were productive or no shows that you are indifferent to the wrong of usury, and willing to do that wrong under the pretence that it was not your business to inquire."

The attitude of the law on money-lending in the old days was very much what it is today with regard to certain poisonous chemicals which may be used well or ill. The seller of those chemicals has to ask what they are going to be used for, and is responsible if he fails to inquire. In the same way the old Christian law said a lender was bound to find out if his loan were intended for production or not. If the law had not done this, then usury would have been universal and would have eaten up the State, to the profit of the few people who lent out their money: as it is doing now.

But as trade became more and more complicated and much larger and lost its personal character, as the Banking System arose on a large scale and great companies with any number of shareholders, and as it became impossible to lay the weight of proof upon the lender – when, indeed, most lenders could not know for what their money was being lent, but only that they had put it into some financial institution with the object of fructifying it – then the opportunity for usury came in, and it soon permeated all commerce.

Suppose a man today, for instance, to put money into an Insurance Company. It pays him, let us say, 5 percent interest on his money. He does not know, and cannot know – no one can know – exactly how that particular bit of money is being used. It is merged in the whole lump of the funds the Insurance Company has to deal with. A great deal of it will be used productively. It will go to the purchase of steam engines and stores of food, ships, and so on, which in use increase the wealth of the world; and the money spent in buying these things has a perfect right to profit and does no harm to anyone by taking profit. But a certain proportion will be used unproductively. The original investor knows nothing about that, and even the managers of the company know nothing about it.

A client comes to them and says: "I want a loan of a thousand pounds." They are quite unable, under modern conditions, to go into an examination of what he is going to do with it. He gives security and gets his loan. He may be a man in distress who gets it in order to pay his debts, or he may be a man who is going to start a business. The company cannot go into that. It has to make a general rule of so much interest upon what it lends, under the implied supposition, of course, that the loan is normally productive. But the borrower *can* use it unproductively, and often does and intends to do so.

Thus, with a very large volume of impersonal business, the presence of usury is inevitable. But though inevitable, and though therefore the practice of it, being indirect and distant, cannot be imputed to this man or that, usury inevitably produces its disastrous effects, and the modern world is at last coming to feel those effects very sharply.

A few pence lent out at usury some twenty centuries ago would amount now, at compound interest, to more wealth than there is in the whole world; which is a sufficient proof that usury is unjust and, as a permanent trade method, impossible.

The large proportion of usurious payments which are now being made on account of the impersonal and indirect character of nearly all transactions, is beginning to lay such a burden upon the world as a whole that there is danger of a breakdown.

If you keep on taking wealth as though from an increase, when really there is no increase out of which that wealth can come, the process must, sooner or later, come to an end. It is as though you were to claim a hundred bushels of apples every year from an orchard after the orchard had ceased to bear, or as though you were to claim a daily supply of water from a spring which had dried up. The man who would have to pay the apples would have to get them as best he could, but by the time the claim was being made on all the orchards of the world, by the time that usury was asking a million bushels of apples a year, though only half a million were being produced, there would be a jam. The interest would not be forthcoming, and the machinery for collecting it would stop working. Long before it actually stopped, of course, people would find increasing difficulty in getting their interest and increasing trouble would appear in all the commercial world.

Now that is exactly what is beginning to happen today after about two centuries of usury and one century of unrestricted usury. So far we have got out of it by all manner of makeshifts. Those who have borrowed the money and have promised to pay, say, 5 percent, are allowed to change and to pay only 2½ percent. Or, by the process of debasing currency, which I described earlier in this book, the value of the money is changed, so that a man who has been set down to pay, say, a hundred sheep a year, is really only paying 50 or 30 sheep a year. A more drastic method is the method of "writing off" loans altogether – simply saying: "I simply cannot get my interest, and so I must stop asking for it." That is what happens when a Government goes bankrupt, as the Government of Germany has done.

If you look at the usury created by the Great War, you will see this kind of thing going on on all sides. The Governments that were fighting borrowed money from individuals and promised interest upon it. Most of that money was not used productively: it was used for buying wheat and metal, and machinery and the rest, but the wheat was not used to feed workmen who were producing more wealth. It was used to feed soldiers who were producing no wealth, and so were the ships and the metal and the machinery, etc. Therefore when the individuals who had lent the money began collecting from the Government interest upon what they had lent they were asking every year for wealth which simply was not there, and the Governments have got out of their promise to pay a usurious interest in all sorts of ways – some by repudiating, that is saying that they *would not* pay (the Russians have done that), others by debasing currency in various degrees. The English Government has cut down what it promised to pay to about half, and by taxing this it has further reduced it to rather less than a third. The French Government, by inflation and by taxation, have reduced it much more – to less than a fourth, or perhaps more like a sixth or an eighth.

The Germans have reduced it by inflation to pretty well nothing, which is the same really as repudiating the debt altogether.

So what we see in a general survey is this—

1. Usury is both wrong morally and bad for society, *because it is the claim for an increase of wealth which is not really present at all.* It is trying to get something where there is nothing out of which that something can be paid.

2. This action must therefore progressively and increasingly soak up the wealth which men produce into the hands of those who lend money, until at last all the wealth is so soaked up and the process comes to an end.

3. That is what has happened in the case of the modern world, largely through unproductive expenditure on war, which expenditure has been met by borrowing money *and promising interest upon it although the money was not producing any further wealth.*

4. The modern world has therefore reached a limit in this process and the future of usurious investment is in doubt.

Though these conclusions are perfectly clear, it is unfortunately not possible to say that this or that is a way out of our difficulties; that by this or that law we can stop usury in the future and can go back to healthier conditions. Trade is still spread all over the world. It is still impersonal and money continues to be lent out at interest unproductively, with the recurring necessity of repaying the debt and failing to keep up payments which have been promised. Things will not get right again in this respect until society becomes as simple as it used be, and we shall have to go through a pretty bad time before we get back to that.

XII

ECONOMIC IMAGINARIES

I am going to end with a rather difficult subject on which I hesitated whether I should put it into this book or no. If you find it too difficult leave it out; but if you find as you read that you can understand it, it is worth going into, because it is quite new (you will not find it in any other book), and it is very useful in helping one to understand certain difficult problems which have arisen in our modern society and which have become a danger today. This subject is what I call "Economic Imaginaries."

An imaginary is a term taken from mathematics, and means a value which appears on paper but has no real existence. It would be too long and much too puzzling to explain what imaginaries in mathematics are, but I can give you a very simple example of what they are in Economics. They mean economic values or lumps of wealth which appear on paper when you are making calculations, so that one would think the wealth was really there, but which when you go closely into their nature you find do not really exist.

The first example I will give you is that of a man who, having a large income, gives an allowance to his son living somewhere abroad. Supposing a man in England has £10,000 a year, and he has put his son into business in Paris, but because the young man has not yet learned his business, and is still being helped from home, he allows that son £1,000 a year to spend.

When the Income Tax people go round finding out what everybody has they put down the rich man in England, quite rightly, as having £10,000 a year, and when the value of all incomes in England is *assessed*, i.e., when a table is drawn up showing what the total income of all Englishmen is, this man appears, quite properly, as having £10,000 a year. But when the people in France make a similar *assessment,* to find out what the incomes are of all the people living in France, the rich man's son in Paris appears as having £1,000 a year. So when the assessments of England and France are added together and some Government economist is calculating what the total income of the citizens of both countries may be, *that £1,000 a year appears twice.* One of these appearances is an Economic Imaginary. In other words, by the method of calculation used, £1,000 every year appears on the total assessment of England and also of France, making £2,000 of £1,000. The extra £1,000, though appearing on paper, does not really exist at all: it is an "Economic Imaginary."

This is the simplest case of an Economic Imaginary. It is the case overlap, or counting of the same money twice, and we may put down this case in general terms by saying:

EVERY UNCHECKED OVERLAP CREATES AN ECO-
NOMIC IMAGINARY TO THE EXTENT OF THAT UNCHECKED
OVERLAP.

It looks so simple that one might say, "Well, surely everybody would notice that!" But it is very much the other way – even in this simple case. The more complicated society becomes, the more payments there are back and forth, allowances and pensions and all sorts of arrangements which grow up with increased travel and means of communication and, in general, with the development of society, the more these overlaps come into being and remain unchecked, that is, uncorrected, the greater number there are in which people are not aware that there is an overlap, or if it is an overlap do not remember to mention it, or if they do mention it are not believed. In general the more society increases in complexity the more this kind of economic imaginary by mere overlap increases in proportion to the total real wealth, and the more the total "assessment" of the community is exaggerated.

I will give you one instance, to prove this, which is very striking and which happened in my own experience. A man I knew gave in his income tax returns a few years ago. He had a secretary at home to whom he paid a fairly large salary, and he also used a secretary in town. Their salaries came out of money which he had earned in business but appeared in his taxable general income, for he was not allowed to take it off as an expense. Meanwhile, both the secretary in the country and the secretary in town were paying tax on *their* salaries, though they came out of a total income which had already paid taxes, and anyone making an assessment of the total income of England would certainly have written down from the official books: "Mr. Blank, so much a year; his secretary A——, so much a year; his secretary B——, so much a year," and added up the total. Yet it is clear that the money put down to A and B was imaginary.

I cannot tell you the thousands of ways in which this simple case of overlapping goes on in modern England, for it would be too long to explain, and I have only given you very simple instances, but you may be certain that the economic imaginaries of this kind form at least a quarter of the supposed income of the country.

If there were no other form of imaginaries than this it would be very simple to understand them, and perhaps allow for them in making an estimate of total wealth. Unfortunately, there are any number of different forms much more difficult to seize and cropping up like mushrooms everywhere more and more in a complicated and active society.

For instance: you have (2) the economic imaginary due to *luxurious expenditure.*

All over the world where you have rich people spending money foolishly they are asked, for things that they buy, prices altogether out of keeping with the real value of the things. If you go into one of the big hotels in London or Paris and have a dinner the *economic values* you consume are anything from a quarter to a tenth of the sum you are asked to pay. Thus people who buy a bottle of champagne in this sort of place pay from a pound to thirty shillings. The economic values contained in a bottle of champagne, that is the economic values which are built up by the labour of all sorts which has been expended in producing it, come to about two shillings and sixpence. So when people pay from a pound to thirty shillings for a bottle of champagne they are paying from eight to twelve times the real economic values which are destroyed in consumption. There is an extra margin of anything from seventeen shillings and sixpence to twenty-seven shillings and sixpence, which is an economic imaginary in that one case alone. And remember that this economic imaginary goes the rounds. It appears in the profits of the hotel keeper, which are assessed in the total national income for taxation. It appears in the rent for his hotel, since a man will pay much more rent for a house in which he can get people to pay these sums than for a humbler hotel of the same size and of the same true economic value in bricks and mortar. It appears in the rates which the hotel pays to the local authorities, and which in their turn appear in the income of humble officials living in the suburbs. That economic imaginary created by the silly person who is willing to pay from a pound to thirty shillings for a thing worth two shillings and sixpence appears over and over again in the various assessments of the country.

Here is another case (3): *economic imaginaries due to inequality of income.*

Supposing you have a thousand families with £1,000 a year each; that is, a total income among them of £1,000,000 a year. Supposing you put up for competition among those families a very beautiful picture which everybody would like to have; painted, say, by Van Dyck. None of these people with £1,000 a year each could afford to give more than a certain sum for the picture, and probably, when they had competed for it, it would fetch no more than £100. An official estimating that community would say that it had £1,000,000 a year income, such and such values in houses, etc., and that there was a picture present worth £100, and all that would go down in his estimates or "Assessment."

Now supposing all but two of these thousand families to be impoverished by having to pay rents and interest to these two men. Supposing they were all reduced to just under £500 a year, and that the balance of £500,000 were paid to those other two. Then each of these would have £250,000 a year. The Van Dyck is put up for auction in this community. The poor families, of course, have no show at all. Not one of them can afford more than £50 at the most, however much he wanted the Van Dyck. But the two rich men can compete one against the other recklessly. They have an enormous margin of wealth with which to do what they like, and the Van Dyck between them may be rushed up to £50,000.

There is not a penny more of real wealth in the community than there was before. Yet your Government assessor would come down and assess the community in a very different fashion from the way in

which he would have assessed the first community. He will put down
the total income at £1,000,000, and the houses, furniture, etc., at so
much, and he will add: "Also a Van Dyck valued at £50,000." Of
course in real life, where are great differences of income, this sort of
thing is multiplied by the thousand. It is another example of the way
in which, as communities get more complicated in a high civilisation,
economic imaginaries appear.

I am only introducing this subject as a very simple addition to
this little book, and I will not multiply instances too much, though
one might go on giving examples almost indefinitely.

Here, then, is a last one (4): *economic imaginaries due to the confusion between services and economic values attached to material things.*

We saw at the beginning of this book that wealth did not
consist in *things,* such as coal, chairs, tables, etc., but in the *economic
values attached to those things;* that is, their added use for the purposes
of human beings up to the point where they were beginning to be
consumed. We saw how the coal in the earth has no economic value,
how it begins to be of value when it begins to be mined, and how each
piece of additional labour put into it to bring it nearer to the point of
consumption adds to its economic value, until at last, when it gets
into your cellar, from being worth nothing a ton (when it was still in
the earth) it is worth thirty shillings or forty shillings a ton.

But when people assess wealth for the purpose of taxation, and
in order to find what (in their judgment) the total yearly income of a
nation is, they count not only the economic values attached to things
consumed by the nation, but also *services.*

For instance: if Jones is a good card player, the rich man Smith
may pay him £500 a year to live in his house and amuse his loneliness by perpetually playing cards with him. I knew a case of a man
in South Wales who did exactly that. It is an extreme case, but we
all of us, all day long, are paying money for services which do not
add economic values to things at all, and which yet must appear in
assessment.

All the money I earn by writing is of this kind. Now assessment
of these services creates an enormous body of economic imaginaries,
and to show you how they may do so I will give you an extreme and
ludicrous case.

Supposing two men, one of whom, Smith, has a loaf of bread, and the other of whom, Brown, has nothing. Smith says to Brown: "If you will sing me a song I will give you my loaf of bread." Brown sings his song and Smith hands over the bread. A little later Brown wants to hear Smith sing and he says to him: "If you will sing me a song I will give you this loaf of bread." A little later Smith again wants to have a song from Brown. Brown sings his song (let us hope a new one!) and the loaf of bread again changes hands and so on all day.

Supposing each of these transactions to be recorded in a book of accounts. There will appear in Smith's book: "Paid to Brown for singing songs two hundred loaves of bread," and in Brown's book: "Paid to Smith for singing songs two hundred loaves of bread." The official who has to assess the national income will laboriously copy these figures into his book and will put down: "Daily income of Smith, 200 loaves of bread. Daily income of Brown, 200 loaves of bread. Total 400 loaves of bread." Yet there is only one *real* loaf of bread there all the time! The other 399 are imaginary.

Now with a ludicrous and extreme example of this sort you may say: "That is all very well as a joke, but it has no bearing on real life." It has. That is exactly the sort of thing which is going on the whole time in a highly-developed economic society. I go to a matinee and pay 10s. for a man to amuse me. He goes off himself in the evening and pays 10s. to hear a man sing at a concert. Next morning that man (I sincerely hope) buys one of my books, and a big part of the price is not paid for the economic values attaching to the material of it, but for the services of writing it, which is not a creation of wealth at all. The publisher pays me my royalty, and I spend part of it in looking at an acrobat in a music hall. The acrobat pays 10s. to keep up his chapel; and the minister of the chapel, in a fit of fervour, pays a subscription of 10s. to a political party.

And so on. Here is a short chain of economic imaginaries: 50s. – five ten shilling notes – all appearing one after the other in the assessment of the national income and corresponding to no real wealth.

It is exactly the same thing in principle as the case of the two men singing for one loaf of bread. And the same principle applies to the expenditure of rates and taxes. A great part of this expenditure goes in empty services, not in services which add economic values to things.

We must, of course, distinguish between two things which many of the older economists muddled up. A thing may be of the highest temporal use to humanity in the production of happiness, such as good singing, or of high spiritual value, such as good conduct, and yet that thing must not be confounded with economic values. When one says, for instance, that good singing, or a good picture, or a good book has no economic value, or only a very slight material economic value (the best picture ever painted has probably not a true economic value of more than 20s. outside its frame, unless the painter used expensive paints or a quite enormous canvas) one does not mean, as too many foolish people imagine, that *therefore* one ought not to have good singing, or good pictures, or the rest of it.

What *is* meant is that the examination of any one set of things must be kept separate from the examination of another, and when you put down the money spent on these things as though it represented real economic values you are making a false calculation.

Well, this is only a hint of quite a new subject in Economics, which I have put in at the end in the hope that it may be of some value to you. Meditate upon it. As societies get more and more luxurious, more and more complicated, more and more "civilised" (as we call it), so do these economic imaginaries grow out of all proportion to the real wealth of the society. If on the top of their growth you suddenly impose high taxation, based upon your assessment, you may think that you are only taking a fifth or a third or a fourth of the whole community's real yearly wealth, when in reality you are taking a half or more than a half. And this is probably the main reason why so many highly developed societies have broken down towards the end of their brilliance through the demands of their tax-gatherers who worked on assessment inflated out of all reality by a mass of economic imaginaries.

About IHS Press

IHS Press believes that the key to the restoration of Catholic Society is the recovery and the implementation of the wisdom our Fathers in the Faith possessed so fully less than a century ago. At a time when numerous ideologies were competing for supremacy, these men articulated, with precision and vigor, and *without* apology or compromise, the only genuine alternative to the then- (and still-) prevailing currents of thought: value-free and yet bureaucratic "progressivism" on the one hand, and the rehashed, *laissez-faire* free-for-all of "conservatism" on the other. That alternative is the Social Teaching of the Catholic Church.

Catholic Social Teaching offers the solutions to the political, economic, and social problems that plague modern society; problems that stem from the false principles of the Reformation, Renaissance, and Revolution, and which are exacerbated by the industrialization and the secularization of society that has continued for several centuries. Defending, explaining, and applying this Teaching was the business of the great Social Catholics of last century. Unfortunately, much of their work is today both unknown and unavailable.

Thus, IHS Press was founded in September of 2001A.D. as the only publisher dedicated exclusively to the Social Teaching of the Church, helping Catholics of the third millennium pick up where those of last century left off. IHS Press is committed to recovering, and *helping others to rediscover,* the valuable works of the Catholic economists, historians, and social critics. To that end, IHS Press is in the business of issuing critical editions of works on society, politics, and economics by writers, thinkers, and men of action such as Hilaire Belloc, Gilbert Chesterton, Arthur Penty, Fr. Vincent McNabb, Fr. Denis Fahey, Jean Ousset, Amintore Fanfani, George O'Brien, and others, making the wisdom they contain available to the current generation.

It is the aim of IHS Press to issue these vitally important works in high-quality volumes and at reasonable prices, to enable the widest possible audience to acquire, enjoy, and benefit from them. Such an undertaking cannot be maintained without the support of generous benefactors. With that in mind, IHS Press was constituted as a not-for-profit corporation which is exempt from federal tax according to Section 501(c)(3) of the United States Internal Revenue Code. Donations to IHS Press are, therefore, tax deductible, and are especially welcome to support its continued operation, and to help it with the publication of new titles and the more widespread dissemination of those already in print.

For more information, contact us at:

info@ihspress.com • www.ihspress.com • 877-IHS-PRES (447.7737)

IHS Press is a tax-exempt 501(c)(3) corporation; EIN: 54-2057581. Applicable documentation is available upon request.

Titles New & Old from IHS Press

are available direct from the publisher or at fine bookstores.

Order yours today. _____

Order direct today: by phone, fax, mail, e-mail, online.
s/h: $3.50 per book; $1.00 ea. add'l. book. Check, m.o., VISA, MC.

toll-free telephone or fax: 877-IHS-PRES (877.447.7737)
e-mail: order@ihspress.com • *internet:* www.ihspress.com